THE COMPLETE GUIDE TO
SAUSAGE
MAKING

THE COMPLETE GUIDE TO
SAUSAGE MAKING

Mastering the Art of Homemade Bratwurst,
Bologna, Pepperoni, Salami, and More

MONTE BURCH

Skyhorse Publishing

Skyhorse Publishing books may be purchased in bulk at
special discounts for sales promotion, corporate gifts, fund-
raising, or educational purposes. Special editions can also
be created to specifications. For details, contact the Special
Sales Department, Skyhorse Publishing, 307 West 36th
Street, 11th Floor, New York, NY 10018 or info@skyhorse-
publishing.com.

www.skyhorsepublishing.com

10 9 8 7 6 5 4 3 2 1

Library of Congress Cataloging-in-Publication Data is available on file.
ISBN: 978-1-61608-128-7

Printed in China

Contents

Introduction

Home sausage making is a fun, interesting, and satisfying endeavor. It can be a hobby, a means of saving money, a way of creating foods that are suited to your lifestyle, and a way to control the quality of the foods you and your family consume.

Our family has been making sausage for generations. Growing up on a farm in Missouri, I well remember butchering days and the taste of fresh pork sausage. After working for a few years in the city, my wife, Joan, and I eventually acquired and moved to our own farm. Home butchering pigs, cattle, and chickens once again became a way of life. Then came the proliferation of white-tailed deer in the Ozarks, and venison became a staple food for our growing family. Turning venison into jerky and summer sausage was the next step in sausage making. We soon discovered other sausage recipes, such as making our own bologna, braunschweiger, and others, all great uses for homegrown venison and pork.

You can make your own sausage from any number of recipes; there are literally thousands from all over the world, many handed down from generation to generation. In addition to the basics of sausage making, this book also includes recipes for a variety of different types of sausage. Experimenting with seasonings and meat mixes is half the fun, so use these recipes as a guide to the basic ingredients as you create your own repertoire of sausage recipes.

Some sausages are easy to make, while others take quite a bit of effort and not a few tools. Yet when you are able to serve your family and friends great-tasting home-made sausages, you'll experience a great deal of satisfaction knowing exactly what's in the food you are serving.

CHAPTER 1

All About Sausage

THE HISTORY OF SAUSAGE

Known as a staple food for almost a thousand years before Christ, sausage is one of mankind's oldest forms of processed foods. Homer's *The Odyssey* describes a form of sausage made from a goat stomach filled with fat and blood, roasted over an open fire. A Chinese sausage made of lamb and goat meat, called *lachang*, is recorded as early as 589 BC. The word *sausage* comes from the Latin word *salsus*, meaning salted or preserved; *salsus* was an extremely common food for the Romans. Sausages became so popular during the beginning of the Christian era that Roman emperor Constantine banned them.

National varieties of sausage originated in various regions and cities. Sausages are made with herbs, spices, and meats and include traditional ingredients that create special regional dishes. Through the Middle Ages, the

English called it "sausage." In France, the term is *sausis-sons*, and in Germany, *wurst*. During the Middle Ages, sausage making became an art, with numerous commercial sausage makers scattered throughout Europe. In fact, these *wurstmachers*, as they were called in Germany, produced a number of distinctively flavored and spiced sausages that became known by the names of the cities or regions from which they originated and eventually became world famous.

The extremely popular frankfurter, or hot dog, came from Frankfurt, Germany. The *wiener*, however, is a product of Austria, the word meaning "Viennese" in German. Almost as popular, the luncheon meat bologna

Sausage, in all its varieties, is one of mankind's oldest and most important foods. Making your own sausage is not only an enjoyable hobby but also a valuable skill that can provide delicious food for your table.

came from Bologna, Italy. Other famous sausages with city names include Arles, from France; Goteborg summer sausage, from Sweden; Genoa salami, from Italy; and braunschweiger, from Brunswick, Germany. With over 1,500 varieties of *wurst*, Germany has to be the sausage capital of the world. Sausage making was and is a serious business in Germany. During the fifteenth century, the Bratwurst Purity Law outlawed the use of rotten or wormy meat. Other famous German sausages include rindswurst, knockwurst, and bockwurst.

Sausages are also a very popular breakfast dish in the United Kingdom and Ireland, with well over 400 known recipes. A sausage, dipped and fried, is very common in Britain, as is "saveloy," a precooked sausage similar to (but larger than) the hot dog. Colored with brown dye, the sausage has a very distinct red color. A very popular snack food is the "pig in a blanket," a sausage cooked in a pastry. Another version is "toad in the hole," or sausage baked in Yorkshire pudding and served with onions and gravy. Square sausage is a popular breakfast food in Scotland. Seasoned mostly with pepper, it is formed into a block and cut into slices for cooking.

Scottish "black pudding" is similar to German and Polish blood sausages. The national sausage of Switzerland is *cervelat*, a cooked type of summer sausage. *Falukorv*, a traditional Swedish sausage, is made of pork and veal and contains potato flour and mild spices. It originated from the city of Falun. A fermented sausage called *sucuk* comes from Turkey and the neighboring Balkans.

It is made primarily from beef and is placed in an inedible casing that is removed before consuming. Some varieties may also contain sheep fat, chicken, water buffalo, or turkey meat.

Chorizo, a fresh sausage made of beef or pork salivary glands, is the most popular sausage of Mexico. It is often fairly dry, loose, and crumbly and used as a filling for torta sandwiches, tacos, and burritos. A moister and fresher version of chorizo is very popular in much of Latin America. A number of Philippine sausages include varieties of *longaniza* and chorizo. The traditional sausage of South Africa is called *boerewors,* or "farmer's sausage," and is made of game and beef with pork or lamb and usually contains fairly high amounts of fat. In Australia, English-style sausages called "snags" are popular, as is "devon," a pork sausage quite similar to bologna. New Zealand sausages are similar to those from England.

In Asia, popular sausages include Chinese *lap chong,* a dried-pork sausage that has some of the flavor and appearance of pepperoni; a ground-fish sausage from Japan; and *sundae,* a blood sausage and popular street food from Korea. *Saucisson* from France is a dried sausage, containing pork, wine, and/or spirits and salt. A number of regional varieties are made. Italian sausages are typically made of pork only and usually contain fennel seeds, black pepper, and sometimes chilies or parsley. Swedish sausages are also typically made of mostly fine-ground pork and are lightly spiced. In Denmark, the popular "hot dog stand" serves *polser,* a very popular national dish. In

Iceland, traditional sausages have been made of mutton and horse meat. Poland is well known for its variety of sausages, beginning with wild game meat from the royal hunting excursions. The sausages of Portugal, Spain, and Brazil, called *embutidos* or *enchidos*, are often highly spiced with peppers, paprika, garlic, rosemary, nutmeg, ginger, and thyme.

Early immigrants brought the tradition of sausage making to America; it eventually became a very important industry and remains so today. Native Americans had already learned to dry and cure meat such as venison,

Sausage is made from many different types of meat, using many different recipes. A common example of fresh sausage is breakfast patties.

elk, and buffalo, and they also made a sort of sausage, combining spices, berries, and other ingredients with dried meat into a food product called pemmican.

The hot dog is America's favorite sausage, with the corn dog (a hot dog fried in cornmeal) also popular. Pork breakfast sausage in its many varieties is another favorite. America's melting-pot population enjoys a wide variety of sausage, including bratwurst, salami, Italian and

Polish sausages, American-style bologna, liverwurst, head cheese, Cajun boudin, chorizo, and andouille.

TYPES OF SAUSAGES

Sausage is typically made from ground, minced, or emulsified meat. The meat may come from a single species, such as fresh pork sausage, or a combination of several different species, as in the case of hot dogs, bologna, summer

Another very popular type of sausage is dried or hard sausage, often called summer sausage because in some forms it does not require refrigeration. Wild game meat such as venison is often made into summer sausage, but beef and pork are also commonly used.

Cooked sausages are some of the most popular and include traditional hot dogs, bologna, braunschweiger, and other luncheon meats. Making your own is fun and a great way to use a variety of meats.

sausages, and so forth. Almost any type of meat from domestic animals—mutton, goat, beef, pork, and fowl, such as chicken and turkey—to all types of wild game and fish can be made into sausage. Different types of sausages can utilize almost all parts of the animal, which is the main reason for the popularity of sausage through the ages. As my grandmother used to say during hog-butchering days, "We use everything from the pig but the squeal."

Different types of sausages were developed in certain areas because of the types of meat that were found there. Sausages are seasoned in numerous ways, and the recipes are handed down through the generations, with the different recipes providing the variety of flavors. The meat is then cooked into patties or loaves or stuffed into casings. The casings can be either natural (made from animal intestines), artificial, collagen, synthetic, or sewn muslin.

Other common forms are the specialty sausages, many of which, such as liver loaf and head cheese, are made into loaves and baked.

Sausage is available in thousands of varieties worldwide, with different nationalities classifying them differently. In North America and other English-speaking countries, sausage is classified as three basic types: 1) fresh; 2) dry, summer, or hard sausage; and 3) cooked sausage. In other countries, the categories may be expanded to include fresh, fresh/smoked, dry, cooked, cooked/smoked, and so forth.

Fresh sausage is made from meat that is uncured and uncooked, and it must always be cooked before eating. Fresh sausage must also be consumed immediately or kept frozen. It won't keep any longer than fresh meat, even with refrigeration. In many parts of the world, the different forms of fresh sausage are often called breakfast sausage. The most common type of fresh sausage is pork, and even then, there are many different recipes, depending mostly on the flavorings used. Lean wild game meat such as venison and elk are also sometimes mixed with pork fat to create a fresh sausage. Fresh sausage may or may not be stuffed into casings. Stuffed fresh sausage includes bratwurst and other varieties, like Italian and Polish sausages.

Dry or *hard sausage* is sometimes called summer sausage because some types will keep during the summer or during warm weather without refrigeration. This was a very important means of preserving food before refrigeration and canning became available. These sausages are usually eaten cold. In some instances they are also fermented. Summer sausage is sometimes called "seminary" sausage because it is associated with monasteries. Dry sausage is made from cured meat that is either air-dried or commercially dried under controlled time, temperature, and humidity. Examples of dried sausage include salami, pepperoni, and the different varieties of summer sausage.

Cooked sausage is made of fresh meats that are already cooked, meaning they do not have to be cooked again before eating. These may or may not be smoked and include the very popular hot dogs and bologna and the many varieties of meat-and-spice mixtures, like pickle loaf. Although hot dogs do not have to be cooked, most people prefer to heat them before eating. Other examples include braunschweiger and liver sausage.

All types of sausages may or may not be cold-smoked for flavor. In addition to the three basic types, a wide range of specialty sausages exists, and the meats may be uncured or cured, chopped or comminuted. These are usually baked or cooked instead of smoked and formed into loaves. They are commonly served cold on salads and sandwiches and include such things as head cheese. Scrapple, another specialty sausage, is served as a breakfast meat.

Making your own sausage is an ancient skill that is fun to do. Using our guide, you can make up your own meat products with confidence, knowing exactly what's in them and how they are made.

CHAPTER 2

Tools and Materials

You can make sausage with little more than a mixing bowl and basic kitchen measuring tools, including a scale, measuring spoons, and spatulas. Simply purchase ground meat and add seasonings, then cook. But that really isn't sausage making. You'll probably want to be able to grind the meat, stuff the sausages, and cook or smoke them. All of these tasks require some specialized tools, in addition to the kitchen tools you may already have on hand.

You'll need a good, sharp knife for cutting meat. Having more than one knife definitely makes the different meat-cutting chores easier. The best way is to have a number of knives on hand in a variety of shapes for the many different tasks involved.

Although you can make sausage with nothing more than a few kitchen tools, serious sausage making requires a bit more equipment.

It's best to have a variety of knives available. From left to right: butcher knives, a hunting knife with gut hook for field-dressing, a thin-bladed boning knife, and two old-time skinning knives. Each type performs a specific task.

This is especially true if you do your own butchering as well. If you field-dress and skin big game, a skinning knife with a fairly short blade and a gut hook makes field-dressing and skinning easier. The blade shape should be rounded and with a drop point to make it easier to slice the skin from the muscle without cutting the skin. The same fairly short knife can also be used for cutting up the meat during the butchering process, but regular butcher knives, with longer blades, are best for this chore.

I inherited a number of old-time butcher knives, including some that were actually carried by trappers and

The RedHead Deluxe Butcher Knives Kit has a selection of knives suited to specific butchering chores, as well as a meat cleaver, meat saw, and sharpening steel.

explorers back in the 1800s, and I still enjoy using them. Butcher knives come in a wide variety of sizes and shapes, and again, the different types are used for different chores. Wide-bladed knives are best for slicing meat into the small chunks necessary to run them through a grinder for sausage. Thin-bladed, more flexible knives are best to use when deboning meat for jerky. I actually prefer the rounded-tip butcher knives to those with a sharp tip for cutting meat into smaller pieces. The upswept tip doesn't "catch" on meat as you slice it.

You can also purchase butcher knife sets with a variety of knife shapes included. Some sets even include a sharpening steel as well. For instance, the RedHead Deluxe Butcher Knives Kit includes a paring knife, boning knife, butcher knife, meat cleaver, spring shears, square tube saw, honing steel, cutting board, butcher's apron, and six pairs of gloves, all in a carrying case.

It is important to always purchase and use quality knives. Not only are they easier to use, but they are also safer, because they will keep an edge longer and are easier to sharpen. When purchasing a new knife, you should ensure the blade has a sharp edge and resists dulling but is also easy to sharpen.

A variety of handle shapes and materials are used in knife construction. In quality knives, the handles will be most commonly made of hardwood or a synthetic material. The latter handles, sometimes made of soft-molded materials, are easy on the hands for long periods of use.

It's important to understand the types of steel used in knives. Knife blades are made of three different types of steel: carbon, stainless steel, and high-carbon stainless steel. Carbon was the original steel used in knife construction, and many old carbon-steel knives are still in use, including several in my collection. Carbon steel is relatively soft and sharpens very easily, even with nothing more than a handheld stone. It doesn't, however, hold an edge very well and must be continually resharpened. Carbon steel also rusts badly, even if the metal is dried after cleaning. One solution is to spray the metal with a light dusting of spray cooking oil before storage. Always wash the knife thoroughly before reusing to remove any residual oil and rust.

Pure stainless steel is the hardest of the three metals, but it is almost impossible to resharpen correctly at home. Stainless steel will, however, hold an edge nearly forever once sharpened, and it does not rust. The majority of the knife blades today are made from high-carbon stainless steel. This material provides the best of both worlds: It is a fairly easily sharpened blade that will hold an edge for a reasonable length of time, and it doesn't rust as badly as carbon steel.

Knife-blade edges are commonly ground into one of three shapes: flat-ground, hollow-ground, and taper-ground. Flat-ground blades have their edge ground evenly from the back of the blade to the front of the blade and from the heel to the point, then an edge ground. These blades are sturdy and easily sharpened. Hollow-ground edges have a portion of the blade just behind the edge thinned. This creates less drag, but it also creates a weak area in the blade. A better solution is a taper-ground knife. In this case, after the flat grind, an additional grind is made to thin out the blade but not to create the thinness of a hollow-ground edge. A taper-ground produces a knife with less drag, but with a stronger edge than a hollow-ground, and is found only on high-quality knives.

SHARPENING

Keeping knife blades sharp is an extremely important facet of any type of meat preparation. Using the proper tools can make it easier to have sharp knives as needed. Many

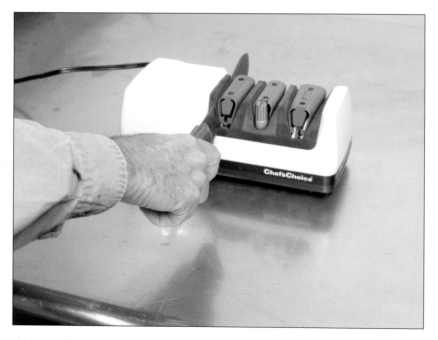

It's extremely important to keep knives sharp. A variety of sharpening devices are available. I've tested several Chef'sChoice power sharpener/hones for a number of years. They are extremely efficient, producing razor-sharp edges in seconds. Shown here is the Model 130.

The Chef'sChoice Diamond Hone AngleSelect Sharpener, Model 1520

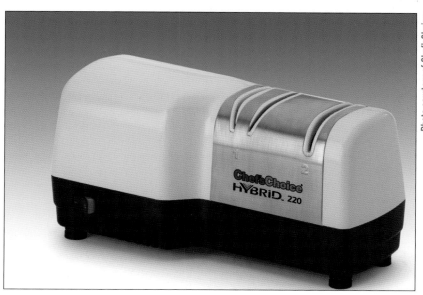

The Chef'sChoice Hybrid Sharpener 220

knife-sharpening devices are available, ranging from the simple but extremely effective butcher's steel to powered sharpeners. Knives that are in good shape other than being dull should never be sharpened using a powered grinder, as you stand a good chance of overheating the steel and losing the temper. Powered sharpening hones, however, can make the chore of sharpening a dull knife quick and easy.

I've tested the Chef'sChoice models for many years. The Chef'sChoice Professional Sharpening Station Model 130 is an excellent choice. It will sharpen both straight and serrated edges and has a 125-watt motor with three sharpening stages: a 40-degree presharpening stage, a 45-degree sharpening stage, and a third steeling stage

One of the best hand-sharpening units I've tested is the Lansky Sharpening System. The system is available in three different kits that consist of hone holders color coded for easy identification of the exact sharpening angles desired.

An old-fashioned butcher's steel is the perfect tool to keep close at hand for regularly retouching the blades of knives as you use them.

for final sharpening. Springs guide the blade for precise sharpening.

Their Model 120 has similar features, except a stropping stage replaces the steeling stage for a Trizor triple-bevel edge.

The Chef'sChoice Diamond Hone AngleSelect Sharpener, Model 1520, is engineered to put a razor-sharp edge on all quality knives and can restore and re-create both a 20-degree edge for European- and American-style knives and a 15-degree edge for Asian-style knives. The multi-beveled, razor-sharp 15-degree edge on hunting knives reduces the amount of effort needed to cut or fillet, making it ideal for skinning and field-dressing.

A more economical sharpener is the Chef'sChoice Hybrid Sharpener. The Hybrid technology combines electric and manual sharpening and features two stages: an electric-powered stage for sharpening and a manual stage for honing. The Hybrid 220 couples the two stages with precise bevel-angle control to provide a super-sharp, arch-shaped edge that is stronger and more durable than the conventional V-shaped or hollow-ground edges.

Another system I've found extremely effective and easy to use is the Lansky Sharpening System. The kit contains finger-grooved hone holders that are color coded for easy identification of the exact sharpening angles desired.

All components are stored in a carrying case: knife clamp with angle selector, guide rods, extra attachment screws, oil, and a sharpening guide. Three kits are available: The Standard Kit has coarse, medium, and fine

Another sharpener to keep on the butcher table is the Lansky Hand Sharpener. A hand guard provides protection for your hand.

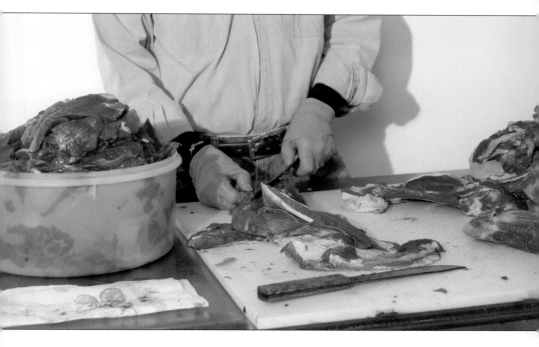

You'll need a nonporous work surface that is easy to clean; a secondhand, stainless-steel table like the one shown here is ideal, or you can use a large synthetic cutting board.

hones; the Deluxe Kit has extra-coarse, coarse, medium, fine, and ultra-fine hones; and the Diamond Kit has coarse, medium, and fine diamond hones. An old-fashioned butcher's steel is actually the quickest and easiest tool to use for keeping an edge on blades as you work. Merely draw the blade across the steel a couple of times as the blade becomes somewhat dull between cuts.

Another extremely simple and efficient sharpener for at-hand work is the Lansky Hand Sharpener. You'll want to keep either of these tools nearby for quick "touch-up" sharpening.

WORK TABLE

These days, in addition to knives, a wide range of tools can make sausage making easier, faster, and safer. Next to a knife, the most important piece of equipment is a good, solid working table or surface that is easily cleaned. Your kitchen table or kitchen countertop will work, but it should not be wood or even the traditional butcher block; instead, it should be an easily cleaned, nonporous surface. Sausage comes out of a stuffer in a fairly long tube, and a large, flat work surface is necessary to catch and hold the sausage.

A number of years ago I purchased a pair of stainless-steel tables at a school auction. These are ideal, as they can be cleaned and sanitized. You can find tables like these quite often when restaurants hold going-out-of-business sales. In lieu of the ultimate table, a large, synthetic cutting board is the next-best option. Regardless of what is used, it must be easily cleaned and sanitized.

GRINDERS

If you're making only a small amount of sausage, a hand grinder may be your best choice. These are economical and easy to use. Of course, they are only as fast as you can hand crank them, and they do require a certain amount of muscle power.

I inherited an old hand grinder, and it had the usual problem of any well-used, well-worn grinder: The blade and plate were dull. In fact, the blade had nicks in it. I

If you have a large amount of ground jerky meat to mix, the LEM 17-pound manual mixer can be a great helpmate.

operate and usually don't produce consistent sausages. If you like to make fresh sausage links with no casings, the LEM Jerky Cannon comes with a nozzle for stuffing sausage and resembles and operates much like a caulking gun.

The next step up is a lever-operated stuffer. This consists of a cast-iron L-shaped tube and lever to push a plunger down through the tube. As I discovered years ago, older models allowed a lot of sausage to escape back past the plunger because of back-pressure from the sausage. Newer models have a rubber or plastic gasket to help prevent this leakage problem around the plunger.

The stainless-steel stuffer is the easiest to fill and use.

Stuffers are available individually or in kits. Kits could include a cast-iron plunger stuffer; seasonings for fresh sausage, summer sausage, and bratwurst; and casings.

Excellent models are available, including cast-iron and 5 lb. stainless-steel models. The stainless-steel models is easier to clean.

To operate, fill the tube and push down on the lever. Vertical stuffers are the easiest to use, with the least amount of hassle, and produce more consistently stuffed sausages—especially when stuffing the smaller-diameter casings.

The LEM stuffer kit includes a 5 lb vertical stainless-steel stuffer; seasoning for 60 lbs of meat, including summer sausage, brats, and flavored sausage; and casings.

These are available in several sizes, including 5 lb., 15 lb., and 25 lb. capacities. All are made of stainless steel, and the cylinder removes for easy cleaning. All come with different-size stuffing tubes.

A larger stuffing kit includes the LEM 5 lb. vertical stainless-steel stuffer; enough Backwoods Seasoning to season sixty pounds of meat, including summer sausage, brats, and flavored sausage (hot, sweet Italian, and hot Italian); ten fibrous casings; two packages of natural hog casings; and a book on making sausage.

Fasten the stuffer to a wooden board that can be clamped to the work surface.

Grinders with stuffing tubes can make grinding and stuffing a one-step process.

Regardless of the stuffer used, it is important it be solidly anchored to the work surface. Fasten the stuffer permanently either to a work surface or to a board clamped to the work surface.

A high-quality grinder such as the LEM model shown also comes with stuffing tubes. You can grind and stuff many sausages at the same time. This is especially true with fresh sausages, when the meat is spiced before grinding.

MISCELLANEOUS

The ends of casings of summer sausage and others can be fastened together with hog rings. For this task, you will need hog rings and hog ring pliers.

To properly mix the ground meat and spices, you'll need a kitchen scale to weigh exact amounts of ground meat. Large and small scales are available, variations of 22 lb. and 44 lb. models are available from most major retailers. Many models comes with a stainless-steel tray and are sufficient to weigh most sausage batches.

We use our office postal scale, which digitally weighs up to 10 pounds and works well for small amounts of ground meats.

Other miscellaneous items needed for sausage making include latex gloves, measuring cups and spoons, glass bowls or other nonmetallic containers, resealable plastic bags or containers, and cookie sheets or racks for drying sausages in an oven.

You will also need a thermometer. The best choice is a digital model with a temperature probe that stays in the meat or sausage when the oven door is closed. An alarm sounds when the desired internal temperature is reached.

Many synthetic casings are fastened with hog rings. You will also need a hog-ringing tool.

A food-safe silicone spray can be used to protect and lubricate all parts of grinders and stuffers.

Although you can easily create your own sausage recipes, a wide range of premixes is available from a number of companies.

Cures for curing sausage are also necessary.

Sausages such as hot dogs, bologna, and others benefit from the addition of soy protein concentrate.

SMOKERS

Many sausage products are smoked not only for flavor but in many instances for preservation as well. Any number of

Most sausage recipes require specific amounts of meat. A kitchen-type (or similar) scale is necessary.

Food-safe latex gloves should be used for any field-dressing chores and are also a good safeguard when mixing sausages.

Most sausages require smoking or cooking. A digital thermometer with a remote sensor allows you to determine the internal temperature of the sausages while baking, boiling, or smoke/cooking.

items may be used for smoking. Smoking actually consists of either cold- or hot-smoking. Cold-smoking is used to dry and flavor the meat; hot-smoking is used to cook the meat as well.

Food-safe silicone spray can be used to lubricate and protect grinders and stuffers.

It's easy to make up your own sausage recipe, but you can also purchase premixed seasonings from Hi-Mountain and Bradley, as well as the LEM Backwoods sausage shown. The Sausage Maker, Inc., actually lists seventy-five various premixed seasonings, ranging from andouille sausage to boudin and venison salami.

The Bradley Smoker people also offer a line of cures for making sausages.

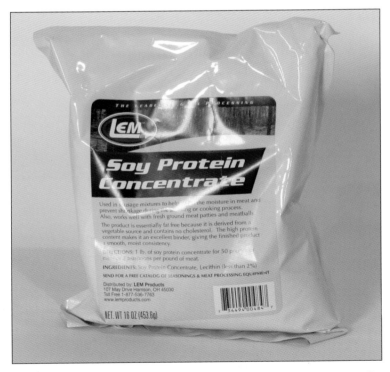

Some sausages also require powdered dextrose or corn syrup, as well as nonfat dry milk or soy protein concentrate.

In the old days wooden smokehouses were a common farmstead building. These were used in late fall or winter to cold-smoke hams, bacon, and sausages. In cold climates some of the smoked meats were left hanging in the smokehouse until consumed. These buildings were usually large enough to allow for a small smoky fire to be built directly inside the structure, usually inside a small stone fire pit, or you could create an outside fire pit and pipe the smoke inside. My granddad had an old smokehouse, and even after he hadn't used it for years, it still held the smell of hickory smoke.

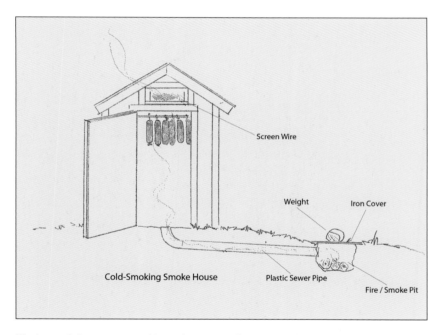

Wooden smokehouses were used to smoke sausages in years past. You can make your own.

Many years ago when I decided to try my hand at cold-smoking meats, I made a smoker from a discarded refrigerator, and it's still extremely effective. A refrigerator smoker can be "fired" in two ways: The first and original method is to cut a hole in the bottom or lower side of the refrigerator and install a metal pipe. The metal pipe runs a few feet away from the refrigerator to a fire pit. The pipe should be buried (or covered with soil) for insulation. A smudge or smoky fire is built in the fire pit, and a sheet-metal cover is placed over the top of the pit to force the smoke into the pipe and refrigerator. A smoke opening must be cut in the top of the refrigerator, and

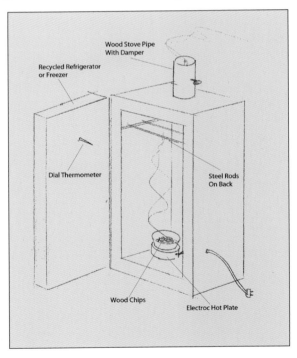

Sausage smokers can also be made from an old refrigerator. This may be fueled by a fire pit or by using an electric hot plate.

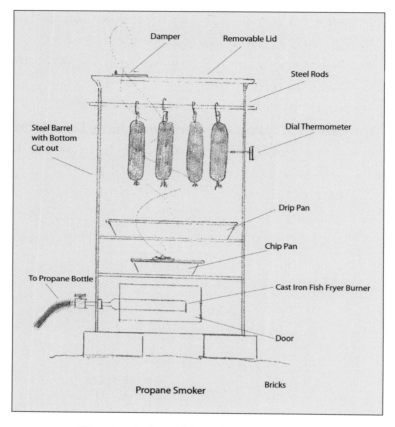

Damper
Removable Lid
Steel Rods
Steel Barrel with Bottom Cut out
Dial Thermometer
Drip Pan
Chip Pan
To Propane Bottle
Cast Iron Fish Fryer Burner
Door
Bricks
Propane Smoker

A barrel smoker is one of the easiest kinds to make.

a damper added. (A woodstove pipe with a damper can be used.)

The last step is to drill a hole near the top of the refrigerator and install a dial meat thermometer with silicone caulking around it. The only problem with both the refrigerator smoker and the old-fashioned smokehouse is that they both require a lot of attention to maintain the correct fire for smoking.

A number of years later, I added an electric hot plate to the bottom of my refrigerator smoker. Placing a pan of wood chips soaked in water on the hot plate made smoking easier, but I still had to monitor the thermometer and refill the chip pan.

You can also make a smoker from a large barrel, fueled by a propane bottle. This smoker can be used for both

Photo courtesy of Bradley Smoker

Electric smokers make smoking sausages easy and precise. The electric Bradley Smoker can heat up to 320°F for serious cooking, or the thermostat can be turned down to 200°F or lower for drying the meat.

cold- and hot-smoking. Fire is provided by a cast-iron fish or turkey fryer burner with regulator. You will, of course, need to build a rack to hold the chip pan and water/ grease pan. A dial thermometer, a remote probe thermometer, and a damper on the top of the barrel smoker are also required.

A number of manufactured smokers are on the market these days, and many make smoking sausage much easier and more precise. These range from simple barbecue-style smokers utilizing charcoal to huge smokers capable of smoking a whole hog. The latter are dedicated smokers

Photo courtesy of Bradley Smoker

Bradley also has a cold-smoke adapter accessory that allows you to cold-smoke at lower temperatures.

The Bradley Smoker utilizes compressed wood-chip flavor bisquettes, available in a variety of wood-smoke flavors.

and can be used for cold-smoking and hot-smoking. Actually, the terms are a bit misleading. Pure cold-smoking doesn't cook the meat; it only adds smoke and dries the meat at temperatures under 130°F. Dedicated smokers, however, are primarily used to cook meat, although at a lower temperature and slower than in a direct-heat unit, such as a barbecue grill.

For instance, I smoke rib slabs at 225°F for almost an entire day but at much lower temperatures than you would find in a direct-heat grill. This is still hotter than cold-smoking.

One unit I've used for many years is the Good-One Smoker, and I've just about worn it out. These smokers are all quite expensive, but they can do double duty. Horizon Smokers are an excellent choice, as are the Traeger smokers that utilize nontoxic wood pellets instead of charcoal. These smoke without an open flame.

The best choices for smoking sausage, however, are the electric smokers. One of the units I've used for years is the Bradley Smoker. Although mine is an older unit,

The Masterbuilt Electric Digital Smokehouse is a great choice for sausage makers. It not only has a digital thermometer with a meat probe, but the window also allows you to watch the smoking process.

The Masterbuilt smoker makes it easy to regulate heat for cold-smoking and for cooking.

A wood-chip tray and water pan on the Masterbuilt smoker provides smoke and moisture.

An outside, removable grease tray on the Masterbuilt smoker makes it easy to collect and discard grease.

the newer, digital models offer a number of advantages. Regardless, with either unit you can hot-smoke at up to 320°F or cold-smoke, slow-roast, or dehydrate down to 140°F merely by turning the thermostat to the desired temperature. A unique feature of the Bradley Smoker is that it burns Bradley flavor bisquettes, preformed wood-chip discs that self-load into the smoker. Precise burn time is twenty minutes per bisquette. The insulated smoking cabinet is easy to use at any time of year. Six removable racks accommodate large loads and allow heat and smoke to circulate evenly. The Bradley has an easy, front-loading design.

The most versatile smoker I've ever tested is the Master-built Electric Digital Smokehouse. You can do anything from simple barbecuing to cooking sausages and smoking all types of meats. The digitally controlled electric smoker comes with a meat probe, an inside light, and a glass door. You can actually watch your meat cook and smoke. The push-button digital temperature and time control makes smokehouse cooking as easy as grilling. The thermostat-controlled temperature creates even, consistent smoking from 100° to 275°F. The built-in meat probe helps ensure perfectly cooked food every time and instantly reads the internal temperature of the sausage.

Wood chips are loaded through a convenient side door. The Masterbuilt smoker also features a drip pan and rear-mounted grease pan for easy cleanup. The removable water pan keeps food moist. The four removable, chrome-

A vacuum packer can greatly extend the storage life of frozen sausages.

coated cooking racks have 720.5 square inches for large quantities of food. An air damper controls smoke.

Most sausages need to stay refrigerated or even frozen for longer-term storage. Vacuum-packing with a vacuum packer extends the storage life of your sausage. The better models have storage for the vacuum-bag rolls and a cutter built right into the unit. Vacuum packers are available online and from major retailers.

CHAPTER 3

Food Safety

Any type of food processing requires an understanding of safety issues and careful adherence to safe food-handling methods. This includes utilizing safe foods such as disease-free meat, safe food-handling steps, and safe food processing. Making your own sausage is relatively simple and is, in fact, one of the oldest and most-common forms of meat preservation. Old recipes partnered with modern food-handling methods results in the best of both worlds.

SAFE MEAT

The first prerequisite for safe sausage making at home is safe meat. You should use meat only from healthy, disease-free animals. It's important to be aware of diseases such as CWD (chronic wasting disease), found in wild deer, elk, and moose, and BSE (bovine spongiform encephalopathy), found in beef cattle, as well as the parasitic diseases of toxoplasmosis and trichinosis in hogs, bear, and other wild game. According to the Wildlife Management Institute:

> There is currently no evidence that CWD is transmissible to humans. However, public health officials recommend that human exposure to the CWD agent be avoided as they continue to research the disease. Although the agent that causes CWD has not been positively identified, strong evidence suggests that prions are responsible. Prions are

Meat processing requires that you pay attention to safety precautions. The first is to use meat only from healthy animals, whether wild game or domestic.

abnormally shaped proteins that are not destroyed by cooking. Accordingly, hunters are advised not to eat meat from animals known to be infected with CWD. Research completed to date indicates that prions generally accumulate in certain parts of infected animals—the brain, eyes, spinal cord, lymph nodes, tonsils and spleen.

Based on these findings, hunters in CWD areas are advised to completely bone out harvested cervids in the field and not consume those parts of the animal where prions likely accumulate. Health officials advise hunters not to shoot, handle or consume any animal that is acting abnormally or appears to be sick. In addition, they suggest hunters take normal, simple precautions when field dressing a carcass. A complete list of current hunter recommendations is available at www.CWD-info.org.

Parasitic diseases can also be a problem. Toxoplasmosis is a parasitic infection caused by a protozoan known as *Toxoplasma gondii*. Humans most often become infected by this organism by consuming undercooked meat, especially lamb, pork, and venison, or eating unwashed fruits and vegetables. Cats, both domestic and wild, are often the carriers. A healthy person who becomes infected often experiences few symptoms, but people who have weakened immune systems are at risk of severe complications.

Trichinosis (or trichinellosis) is a disease caused by a parasite called *Trichinella*. According to the Centers for Disease Control and Prevention, National Center for Infectious Diseases, Division of Parasitic Diseases:

> Trichinella species have been found in virtually all warm-blooded animals. It's important to avoid eating undercooked meat of pork, bear, cougar, wild boar, and walrus. Make sure the meat is cooked to an internal temperature of 160°F before consumption. In the past it was thought freezing for thirty days or more killed the parasite, but trichinella in bear meat is not killed by freezing, and some home freezers will not reach the cold

Some wild game, such as boar or bear, can carry diseases such as trichinosis. Make sure all game meat is cooked properly to 160°F, or 165°F for poultry or game birds (internal temperature), before eating.

temperatures needed to kill parasites. Commercial irradiation is used to kill the parasite. Smoking, drying, curing or microwaving does not consistently kill the infective trichinella worms.

Meat that is tainted, unsafely butchered, and then cut up for use also poses serious health problems, especially from *E. coli*. As a kid back in the 1940s, I watched the community butchering process as neighbors came in and everyone worked together to butcher hogs. My dad often told the story about a mishap that occurred when a piece of meat fell off the cutting table and dropped onto the ground where the hog scalding and scraping had occurred, covering the meat with hair. "The one that eats the most sausage gets the most hair," a neighbor joked as the scrap was quickly eaten by the neighbor's dog. Luckily, the dog survived, but you might not.

Food poisoning by *E. coli*, however, is no joke. It's a serious and deadly health problem that can make you extremely ill and can even kill. *E. coli* is a bacterium that commonly lives in the intestines of people and animals. Many strains of *E. coli* exist, and most are normal, nonpathogenic inhabitants of the small intestines and colon. This means they do not cause disease in the intestines. *E. coli 0157:H7*, however, is a dangerous disease-causing bacterium that comes mostly from poorly cooked meat, most commonly hamburger, which is why the illness is often called "hamburger disease."

E. coli causes bloody diarrhea and cramps and a blood and kidney disease in children. The most common cause is contamination of the meat from intestinal fluids that are spilled or smeared on the meat during the field-dressing or butchering process. This is especially true when the meat is then ground, spreading the contamination throughout the meat. Make sure all meat is cooked to 160° F at some point during the sausage-making process.

FIELD-DRESSING

In many instances if you're making sausage from wild game, including deer, elk, or others, you'll be field-dressing and maybe butchering the wild game as well.

There is no reason you shouldn't do all your own processing; it's not complicated, and food safety is not an issue if you follow commonsense safety rules. Use the proper steps in field-dressing and caring for the carcass, and then make sure the meat is processed properly. If you process all your own meat, you will know exactly what you and your family are eating.

Field-dress wild game as soon as possible after it has been killed to allow the body heat to dissipate rapidly. Venison can be heavily contaminated with fecal bacteria; the degree varies with the hunter's skill, the location of the wound, and other factors. Take all necessary steps to avoid puncturing the digestive tract, a common problem caused by not cutting around and tying off the anus during field-dressing or by cutting into the intestines

Unsafe field-dressing of wild game can also be a problem, causing dangerous diseases such as E. coli. *Make sure you field-dress game using all efforts to prevent contamination of the meat with intestinal fluids.*

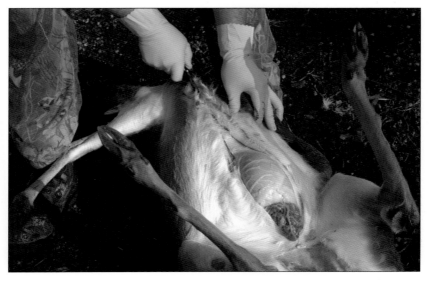

A hunting knife with a gut hook can help to prevent contamination during field-dressing.

when opening the abdominal cavity. A sharp, gut-hook knife helps avoid this problem.

With a gut-shot animal, however, you'll have a problem. Remove as much of the digestive material as possible and thoroughly wash out the cavity with lots of running water. Then, do not use but cut away and discard any meat that has been tainted during the butchering process. Thoroughly clean and disinfect the knife before further use. Do not cut through any organs you suspect might contain disease. The same safety and commonsense cleanliness rules apply when butchering domestic livestock as well.

The carcass must be skinned and chilled as quickly as possible and kept below 45° F to age or until you cut it up.

AGING

If the weather stays suitable, skin and hang the carcass for a few days, but the temperature should not reach above 45°F. Although fresh beef at the slaughterhouse is usually rapidly chilled, deer carcasses are typically held at ambient temperatures, potentially allowing bacteria to multiply. You may wish to allow the carcass to hang for a few days, then skin just before butchering.

If you have an old refrigerator, set it to 35 to 40°F, cut the carcass into quarters, and age in the refrigerator for about a week. Blood will pool on the lower ends, so make sure you place the pieces upright in pans and drain away the excess blood daily. In any case, chill the meat to below 40°F as quickly as possible to ensure the least possible amount of contamination problems.

It is not unusual for our family and friends to have a half dozen deer down on opening day, and here in the Ozarks, the daytime temperature during November can often be in the 70s. Several years ago I found an old "reefer" (refrigerator truck body) that was being used by a restaurant. When they had a going-out-of-business sale, I acquired this ultimate "giant refrigerator" for a couple of hundred bucks, bringing it home with a little help from a buddy with a flatbed trailer. In warm weather we use the unit to hang deer to age, as well as to hold quantities of meat in covered tubs as we process it.

Keeping everything clean and disinfected is a very important step in meat processing. Always wash all working surfaces and tools before and after use with hot soapy water, and then rinse with clean hot water.

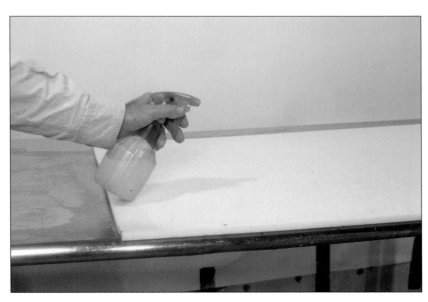

A solution of bleach, water, and soap in a spray bottle can be used to disinfect surfaces and tools.

Cutting boards used with raw meat should not be used for other foods. Always use food-safe gloves when handling sausage meats.

CLEANING AND DISINFECTING

One of the most important facets of all the steps in butchering and meat processing is to keep everything clean and disinfected. This includes work surfaces such as tables, countertops, and cutting boards.

Make sure to thoroughly clean and disinfect knives, grinders, and stuffers, as well as any tools that come into contact with the meat. Clean all surfaces with extremely hot, soapy water with a little bleach added, and rinse with clean hot water. A solution of bleach, soap, and water kept in a spray bottle can also be useful in cleaning surfaces and equipment. Always follow by rinsing with clean hot water. Be sure to clean and sanitize all equipment before and after using and before storing away as well.

Because ground meat has more surface area than whole meat, it is more susceptible to bacteria. Always make sure your hands and nails are scrupulously clean, or wear food-safe gloves while handling, grinding, and mixing sausage meats.

BUTCHERING DEER FOR SAUSAGE

My favorite butchering method for making deer into sausage these days is to bone off all meat while the deer

Boning the meat from the carcass not only avoids cutting through bones and potential pathogen problems but is also easier than using a meat saw. The front shoulder is easily removed by slicing from the carcass.

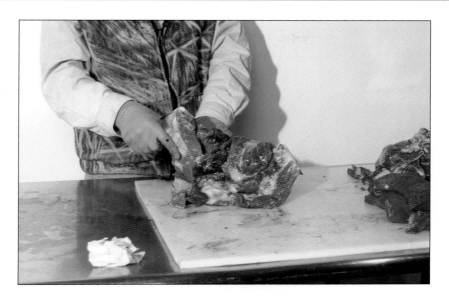

Then simply cut around the bone with a sharp knife to debone.

The shoulder bone has a sharp ridge on one side. Cut in around it to remove the meat.

Continue deboning the carcass. Shown here: cutting off the flank steak.

carcass is still hanging. This prevents the possibility of contamination from pathogens found in the brain and spinal column when cutting through them with a meat saw. This results in a pile of boneless meat, the loins going into the freezer for steaks, and the rest to be ground "burger" or made into sausage, with some used for jerky as well.

The carcass should be hanging head down. The first step is to skin the carcass (if not already done). I like to use a rope winch to lower or raise the carcass as I work on the different areas. The skin can be removed with or without cutting off the head and front feet. One method is to skin down to the head and cut it off at the neck, then skin down to the front feet and cut them off with a meat saw. Or skin

The result is a pile of boneless meat.

Remove the loins by cutting down along the backbone, then making a cut from the rib side and peeling it out.

The loin has a layer of fat on the outside; peel this off.

The backstrap or loin offers a choice piece of meat that can be used for steaks or sliced into muscle-meat jerky.

A layer of tough sinew also covers the loin. Native Americans used this major source of sinew for many items. Using a boning knife, start a cut between the meat and sinew, then turn the loin sinew side down on a smooth flat surface and slice it with a sharp knife, much like filleting a fish.

down to the head and cut off the skin at the joint between the head and neck. Cut from inside the skin to help prevent getting hair on the carcass. Skin down to the hocks and encircle the legs with a cut to remove the skin from the legs. The latter avoids using a meat saw completely, but it requires a bit more skinning effort.

Using a good, sharp boning knife, separate a front shoulder from the carcass. There is no connecting bone joint between the shoulder and the body. Simply pull the front leg out and away from the carcass and slice it off. Lay this shoulder aside and remove the other.

Again, using a good boning knife, simply cut all the meat away from the shoulder bone and leg.

Most sausages must be consumed immediately or frozen for future use. You can also grind and freeze meat and make sausage anytime. Freezing in 1 lb. packages makes it easy to thaw the right amount.

The bottom portion of the leg is filled with sinew and is quite tough. I usually add this to another pile to be used as "dog food" (cooked first) for our Labs, but it can also be ground with a sharp grinder. Note: There is a sharp ridge of bone on the outside of the shoulder that must be cut around to obtain all the meat from the side.

Place these boned-out pieces in a clean, covered tub and refrigerate until you can grind them.

Remove the backstrap or loin by cutting down either side of the backbone, then cutting from the rib side to release the long strip of meat. Properly cut, the loin will peel out fairly simply. Cut away the other backstrap in the same manner. This choice piece of meat can be ground for sausage, but we find that it's just too tasty to eat it grilled. Don't forget to cut and peel the small tenderloin pieces located inside the carcass next to the backbone. Cut away the brisket meat, as well as the layer of meat joining the ribs and the backbone. Then simply cut away all neck meat, leaving the neck bone. This is tougher meat that requires the use of a consistently sharp knife. Although my nephew bones out the meat between each rib, I find this meat has a lot of fat, which must then be trimmed away when grinding, so I usually leave it in place to be discarded with the carcass.

The hams or hindquarters provide the most meat for sausage and are also boned out while the carcass is still hanging. Don't worry about keeping specific pieces separate, such as you would do with labeled, traditional butchering. If there was any spillage of intestinal fluids around the aitch bone or anus area, it would be on the exposed ends of the hindquarters next to the bone. Trim these pieces away, and then wash and sterilize the knife. Make a cut starting at the top of the hindquarter and simply follow the bone down to the aitch bone area. Make a cut down the aitch bone to meet the first cut, then continue cutting around the bone until you have removed all of the meat.

Now you are left with a completely boned-out carcass and a good amount of boneless meat ready to grind for sausage. And there are no bones to take up excess space in your refrigerator or freezer.

Again, these boned-out pieces must be kept well refrigerated until they can be ground for sausage. Do not wait overly long, as even refrigerated meat will spoil. Cut up or grind within three days. Actually, it is suggested that you freeze the meat at 0° to 5°F for sixty days, which will kill most pathogens, except trichinosis in bear meat and hogs.

SLICING AND CHUNKING

The next step is to cut the meat into chunks to be ground. On deer it's important to cut away all the fat and as much gristle and sinew as possible. The former doesn't create a safety problem, but fat in deer adds an "off" taste. The amount of fat trimmed away from beef and pork depends on the type of sausage and your taste preferences. An excess of beef suet can also create an off taste. Trim away all gristle and sinew, as it makes the meat tough, and make

If smoke-cooking sausages, you must use smokers that can attain high-enough heat to cook sausages to an internal temperature of 160° F.

sure you cut away all bloody meat parts and discard them. Always thoroughly wash your hands both before and after you handle raw meat. Do not use cutting boards for both meat and other foods, but keep meat-only boards. Clean and sanitize cutting boards often.

Other important safety steps must also be followed:

- Keep meat and poultry refrigerated below 40°F.
- Use or freeze ground beef and poultry within two days; whole red meats, within three to five days.
- Defrost frozen meat in the refrigerator, not on the counter.
- Marinate meat in the refrigerator, and discard marinades; do not reuse.

COOKING, DRYING, AND SMOKING SAUSAGE SAFELY

Sausages are basically fresh (uncooked), dried, or cooked. Many of the dried or cooked sausages may also be smoked. Fresh or uncooked sausages must be cooked to an internal temperature of 160°F (or 165°F for poultry meat) before consuming. When making cooked sausages, such as frankfurters, they should be cooked after stuffing to an internal temperature of 160°F (165°F for those containing any poultry).

Dry sausages, such as summer sausages or pepperoni, have traditionally not been cooked but are dried. This is where things get a bit confusing. These sausages actually consist of two categories, both dry and semidry sausages. According to the USDA Fact Sheet on Food Safety:

Dry and semidry sausages are possibly the largest category of dried meats, particularly in the United States. These products can be fermented by bacterial growth for preservation and to produce the typical tangy flavor. Alternatively, they may be cultured with lactic acid—such as cheese, pickle and yogurt makers do—to eliminate the fermentation phase and shorten the process. They are, with a few exceptions, cooked.

Fermentation is one of the oldest methods of preserving meats. Dry sausages—such as pepperoni and semidry sausages, such as Lebanon bologna and summer sausage—have had a good safety record for hundreds of years.

In this procedure, a mixture of curing agents, such as salt and sodium nitrite, and a "starter" culture of lactic acid–bacteria, is mixed with chopped and ground meat, placed in casings, fermented, and then dried by a carefully controlled, long, continuous air-drying process. The amount of lactic acid produced during fermentation and the lack of moisture in the finished product after drying typically have been shown to cause pathogenic bacteria to die.

Semidry sausages are usually heated in the smokehouse to fully cook the product and partially dry it. Semidry sausages are semisoft with good keeping qualities due to their lactic acid fermentation and, sometimes, heavy application of smoke.

Some are mildly seasoned and some are quite spicy and strongly flavored.

Dry sausages include Sopressata (a name of a salami), pepperoni (not cooked, air-dried), and Genoa Salami (Italian, usually made from pork, but may have a small amount of beef; it is moistened with wine or grape juice and seasoned with garlic).

Semidry sausages include: summer sausage, Lebanon bologna, Cervelat, and Thuringer.

Some dry sausages are shelfstable (in other words, they do not need to be refrigerated or frozen to be stored safely). Because dry sausages are not cooked, people "at risk" (older adults, very young children, pregnant women, and those with immune systems weakened by disease or organ transplants) might want to avoid eating them. The bacterium *E. coli 157:H7* can survive the process of dry fermenting, and in 1994, some children became ill after eating dry cured salami containing the bacteria. After the outbreak, FSIS developed specific processing rules for making dry sausages that must be followed, or the product must be heat-treated.

Any of the sausages may be smoked for flavor, and some are smoke-cooked as well. Sausages, regardless of the type, must be considered raw or fresh unless they have been heated to an internal temperature of 160°F. For instance, some recipes call for smoking at 100°F for several hours.

This is not a heat treatment but smoking. Regardless of whether you are smoking or drying, the recipes in this book call for a heat treatment of the required internal temperature of 160°F (or 165°F for sausages containing any poultry).

Smokers that can achieve the desired temperatures, and maintain the temperatures properly, should be used. Smoking can also add more flavor to the jerky. Electric smokers with adjustable temperature controls up to 275°F or over are a good choice. Use only proper smoking wood or chips, such as apple, hickory, alder, or mesquite. Softwoods such as pine contain resins and compounds that not only provide an off flavor but are also dangerous.

CHAPTER 4

Sausage Basics

The number of steps involved in sausage making depends on the type of sausage being made. These steps include preparing and grinding the meat; seasoning/mixing; stuffing; and curing, smoking, and/or cooking the sausage.

MEAT PREPARATION

Sausage is traditionally made from meat "scraps" and trimmings from butchering, utilizing many of the meat parts that are considered the less-desirable cuts. For instance, when butchering an animal, you'll have small trimmings from the shoulders, hams, steaks, and so forth. A typical hog will provide about fifteen pounds of trimmings from

Sausages have traditionally been made out of the trimmings from butchering animals. Butchering day at the Burch family farm was usually in January, so the meat would cool down properly and stay cool during the time required to butcher and make the various food products, including sausage.

Good sausage requires some fat; the most common ratio is 75 percent lean meat to 25 percent fat, although the percentage can vary according to taste. In many instances you will need to trim some fat from the lean meat.

these cuts. Other commonly used meats include the neck, feet, heart, liver, tongue, and head.

If you are making any quantity of sausage, you'll need additional meat. Sausage can be made from the entire animal, with whole-hog fresh sausage being especially prized because the entire carcass, including the loins, hams, and shoulders, is utilized. Good sausage normally contains about 75 percent lean meat and 25 percent fat, although this will vary somewhat depending on the recipe and personal preference. Some people prefer a two-third lean and one-third fat combination, while others prefer an 80 to 20 percent mix.

When making sausage of lean meat—such as beef and especially venison—pork fat is usually added. In some countries mutton is used for the fat. Fat allows for easier frying of fresh sausage and helps bind the lean meat in other types of sausage. Fat is especially important when using any extra-dry meat, such as venison. Too much fat, however, can also be a problem. Excess suet should be trimmed from beef, and because of the potentially "gamey" flavor, all fat should be removed from venison. It's also important to keep pork fat levels low in all pork sausages.

The only time I remember my grandparents disagreeing was during hog-butchering days. The Burch family fresh pork sausage was typically made mostly from the shoulders of the hog, with some trimmings from the sides added. The hams were sugar cured. Grandma wanted more of the sides put into the sausage, and Granddad wanted more of the sides to slice and fry and make into bacon. If you aren't butchering your own animals but

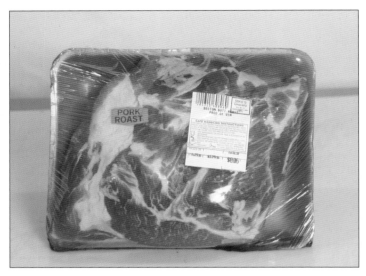

If you purchase meat for sausage, a pork shoulder—called pork "butt" or sometimes "Boston butt"—is a good choice. This cut usually has about the right amount of fat and lean.

You may, however, need to trim some of the outside fat away, and this cut will have a bone. Boning out, however, is not a problem. Make sure you cut in and around the protruding "blade bone" to get all the meat.

A chuck roast or beef plate is the best choice for beef sausage.

Venison is a very popular sausage meat. Make sure you trim away all fat and sinew, as the fat can cause the meat to taste "gamey."

purchasing meat for sausage, many recipes call for "pork butt" or pork shoulders, often called "Boston butt."

A typical bone-in pork shoulder with the skin on will weigh from fifteen to twenty or more pounds. Skinning and deboning will usually result in from thirteen to eighteen or ninteen pounds of meat. A boneless, skinless pork shoulder will provide just about the correct amount of lean meat and fat for a pure pork sausage (i.e., fresh breakfast sausage). However, you may find that you prefer more or less fat content. Regardless, it's important to use only clean, fresh meat ingredients. In most instances when you purchase a pork butt or pork shoulder, it will be bone-in.

Beef trimmings are also traditionally used for sausage making by home butchers. If purchasing beef for making into sausage, economical cuts include chuck roasts and beef plates. A very common meat for deer hunters to use in sausage making is venison. Again, if one is butchering at home, trimmings are used, but successful deer hunters often make "whole-deer" summer sausage, a favorite of ours. With mutton and lamb, the whole carcass is often used for sausage. Turkey and chicken can also be used to make sausage or are often added to other meats to make a less-red-meat type of sausage. Turkey legs are an excellent poultry sausage meat.

Regardless of the meat you use, debone and trim all gristle, sinew, excess suet or fat, and blood spots from the meat. Cut the meat and fat into 1 in. cubes, but keep them separate. Weigh the fat and meat separately and divide into the mixture of fat and meat desired. Then measure all the other ingredients for the sausage recipe being used.

GRINDING

You can have the butcher grind the meat for you, and this is a good choice if you simply want to try your hand at sausage making before purchasing a lot of equipment. But having the meat ground can be costly, and you'll probably want a grinder so you can control the quality of meat and ratio of fat to meat. Meat grinding can be done with a hand grinder or with a powered grinder. The latter, of course, makes the chore easier and faster, and if you prepare any amount of sausage, you'll eventually want to invest in a good electric grinder. Most electric

Serious sausage making requires grinding the meat.

If using different types of meat in a sausage, keep the meats separate. Weigh the trimmed meat and/or fat pieces separately.

Cut the trimmed meat into 1 in. chunks for easier grinding.

grinders can also be equipped with stuffing tubes, making that chore easier as well.

Grinding meat for sausage is fairly easy, but it's a good idea to follow a few basic rules. To maintain the desired ratio of fat and meat, you should weigh the meat and fat and grind together or weigh them into two separate piles or containers and grind separately. Lean meat grinds easier than fat, but in either case, well-chilled meat will grind the easiest. Meat should be 40°F or colder. Make sure there are no bones in the meat to stop an electric grinder or damage the worm gear and grinding plate and blade. A bone will definitely stop a hand grinder and is less likely to damage the grinder.

Grind the meat, making sure you keep the meat cold (40°F or colder). Grinders usually come with two grinding plates with different-size holes, fine and coarse. Different sausage recipes call for using different plates.

Some sausages require finely ground meats. In this case the ground meat should be placed in a flat pan and partially frozen to allow it to firm up.

Feed the meat slowly into the throat of the grinder. Use the meat stomper to push meat into the throat of the grinder head. Do not force the meat, and never use your fingers to push meat into the head. Used properly, today's grinders are very safe, especially compared to older versions, like my granddad's big grinder with a big, wide-open throat. The family joke—"Don't get your tie in there"—was really a reminder to all users to be extremely careful. Make sure you keep the knife and plate sharp and clean. A dull knife or clogged plate tends to crush out the meat juices, retaining more sinew and gristle, slowing or even stopping the grinding process, and reducing the quality of the sausage.

Grind the meat through the coarse (³⁄₁₆ in. or ¼ in.) plate first. Many types of sausage, including fresh, are made from this coarse-ground meat. Actually, any meat product used for frying, such as breakfast sausage, should be coarse ground, or it can become too dry to fry properly.

You may prefer to grind through a finer plate. Some sausages, like bologna and wieners, must be made of finer-ground meat. In this case, the meat is re-ground through the finer-grind (⅛ in.) plate. In some cases you may wish to grind through the fine plate as many as three times.

It's important to rechill the meat for each grind, as the grinding process actually heats up the meat as it goes through the machine. The meat should be

Cut the partially frozen meat into 1 in. chunks and re-grind the chunks.

Repeat if you'd like an even finer grind.

thoroughly chilled after each grind. The best tactic is
to store the coarse-ground meat mixture in a covered
container and refrigerate overnight to allow the meat to
firm up. Another technique to make the grinding even
easier is to soft- or partial-freeze the mixture to about 25° F
and cut into 1 in. cubes. Run these cubes through the
grinder while they are still frozen. Fat grinds best using
the same technique. If you want an even finer meat consistency, again, freeze the meat to 25°F, cut into chunks, and
run through a food processor in small amounts.

With most sausages, the fat is ground last and added
to the mix. This is particularly so with dry, hard sausages
such as salami, which show the fat particles in the sausage
as part of the recipe.

To change to the fine-grind plate, turn off the motor and unplug the grinder. Then, remove the coarse plate and clean the head of the sinew, fat, and gristle that has accumulated during the first grind. There is no way to remove all of this material from the meat scraps; some will always remain and be caught in the grinder. Reassemble the unit with the fine plate, plug in the grinder, and re-grind the meat.

If at any time during the first coarse-grind, or during any of the finer grinds, the meat mashes instead of coming

The ground meat can also be partially frozen, cut into 1-inch chunks, and run through a food processor for emulsifying.

Take the grinder apart and thoroughly clean with hot, soapy water and a bleach/water solution. Spray all parts with a food-grade silicone to prevent rust and to keep your grinder in good condition.

through the plate in "strings," first unplug the grinder; next, remove all meat from the grinder and plate, as well as any sinew that may have collected; reassemble and tighten the grinder ring, tighter than it was previously; and then continue grinding the meat. When you're through grinding, run some saltine crackers through the grinder to help clean out the last bit of meat. (It doesn't hurt if some of the crackers are mixed in with the sausage.)

Once you're through grinding, unplug the grinder and disassemble the grinder head. Wash all parts in hot, soapy water, followed by a bleach/water solution. Rinse thoroughly in hot water. Allow the parts to dry completely. Spray the grinder parts with food-grade silicone to prevent rust and to keep your grinder in like-new condition while stored.

CURING AND SEASONING

All sausages require seasonings, and some also include a cure. The seasonings and cure can be applied to the meat before or after grinding. In the case of fresh or breakfast sausage, the cure and seasonings are sprinkled on the meat chunks before grinding, then the meat, cure, and seasonings are well tossed and stirred before the meat is ground.

Another technique is to mix together the ground meat and ingredients. This is necessary if you utilize previously ground (and often frozen) meat. This method is especially effective if, for instance, you butcher a deer, grind the

Sausages require seasonings, and a wide variety of recipes using different seasonings is available. The simplest method of seasoning sausage is to purchase a prepared seasoning mix.

You can easily make your own sausage seasoning mixes to suit your family's tastes.

In some cases, such as when making certain kinds of fresh sausages, the seasonings are sprinkled on the cut-up meat chunks before grinding.

The seasonings may also be mixed with the ground meat.

meat and then freeze it, and then later accumulate pork or another deer or two to be used with it (or if you wait until you have collected enough other wild game to warrant the time to grind and clean up the grinder). In this case, it's a good idea to package the ground meat in 1 lb. resealable plastic bags or, even better, in vacuum-packed bags and then freeze. You can then get out the varieties of meat in the proportions needed for a specific recipe.

SAUSAGE INGREDIENTS

Besides meat, sausage also requires other ingredients, including salt and spices. Salt is necessary for curing and preservation, and the spices enhance the taste of the sausage. You can purchase the ingredients separately and

Meat cures are also added to some sausages. Use only the amount called for in the recipe.

make up your own blend following any number of recipes, or you can purchase premixed cures and seasonings, ready to use and with "guaranteed" results. The latter are available from a wide range of butcher-supply companies, many on the Internet; you can also get small batches from a local butcher or butcher-supply house.

Nitrates and nitrites have traditionally been used to cure meats, with potassium nitrate (saltpeter) and Prague powder supplying the nitrates and nitrites. According to the National Center for Home Food Preservation:

> Salt is an essential ingredient in sausage. Salt is necessary for flavor, aids in preserving the sausage, and extracts the 'soluble' meat protein at the surface of the meat particles. This film of protein is responsible for binding the sausages together when

chemical change that may occur when certain spices and the curing agents are in contact with each other for an extended period of time. If you do not need an entire package of Morton Sugar Cure (Plain) Mix for a particular recipe or must make more than one application, prepare a smaller amount by blending one and quarter teaspoons of the accompanying spice mix with one cup of unspiced Morton Sugar Cure (Plain) Mix. If any portion of the complete mix with spice is not used within a few days, it should be discarded. It is not necessary to mix the spices with the cure mix if spices are not desired. The Morton Sugar Cure (Plain) mixes contain the curing agents and may be used alone.

Soy protein concentrate is often added to sausages such as hot dogs and bologna as a binder for the finely ground meats.

Another product, Morton Sausage and Meat Loaf Seasoning Mix, is not a curing salt. It is a blend of spices and salt that imparts a delicious flavor to many foods. The seasoning mix can be added to sausage, poultry dressing, meat loaf, and casserole dishes, or it can be rubbed on pork, beef, lamb, and poultry before cooking.

In addition to curing and seasoning agents, many sausage recipes call for additional ingredients, such as starter or fermenting cultures (lactic bacteria) for fermented sausages. Other ingredients include extenders and binders. Commercial sausage makers use extenders to reduce the cost of the sausage, but extenders are not commonly used by home sausage makers. Binders improve the flavor, help retain the natural juiciness, prevent shrinking during smoking or cooking, and provide a finished sausage with a smooth, moist consistency. Nonfat dry milk, cereal flours, and soy protein products are the most commonly used extenders. Soy protein has no taste, contains no cholesterol, and is fat free because it is derived from a vegetable source.

Water is also added to most sausage formulations, and the amount used depends on the type of sausage. Water primarily replaces the moisture lost during smoking and cooking. Approximately 10 percent water is added for moist types of cooked sausage. Fresh sausage is usually made with very small amounts of water, usually less than 3 percent. This only aids in stuffing, mixing, and processing. Dried sausages, such as summer sausage and pepperoni, require no additional water.

MIXING

As you can guess, it's extremely important to thoroughly mix the different meats, cures, and seasonings together. Do not use your bare hands to mix the sausage ingredients; instead, always wear a pair of new, food-safe gloves. If you add cures and seasonings prior to grinding, the ingredients will be pretty well mixed when they come through the grinder. If you add the cures and seasonings after grinding, first mix the different meats (i.e., lean venison and fatty pork) together. Then, add the curing/seasoning ingredients, sprinkling in a little at a time; turn and mix thoroughly; add more and mix again. Overall

It's important to make sure the seasonings and cures are well mixed with the meat. But do not overwork, and make sure to keep the meat cold. Wear clean, food-safe gloves when mixing meat.

mixing time, however, should be fairly short, about three minutes.

Keep the meat cool, or rechill if necessary. A large plastic tub is the best choice for mixing. These are available as meat tubs, or you can substitute large plastic household tubs. Some recipes and techniques call for allowing the cure/seasoning sausage mix to set overnight in the refrigerator; however, this will cause the mixture to set up stiff. If the sausage is to be stuffed, it will be easier to do so if you stuff it as soon as it is ground and mixed with the other ingredients. Salt, as well as other ingredients—like soy protein and nonfat dry milk—all cause the mix to harden.

Fresh sausage is best produced by simply sprinkling on the seasonings, grinding, and stuffing (if it is to be stuffed). An alternative is to simply freeze the fresh

Fresh sausage to be made into patties can be frozen for future use. We press sausage into plastic bowls to achieve a consistent amount of meat, and then place in plastic bags and freeze.

sausage for future use, especially if it is to be cooked as patties. This can be done in two ways: 1) Make up the patties, place waxed paper between them, then place them in a resealable plastic freezer bag. All you need to do is pull out the number of patties you want to cook and add them to the frying pan. 2) Or you can simply place the fresh sausage in resealable bags for freezing.

An even better tactic is to vacuum-pack the sausage, as it will keep longer. It's a good idea to try to keep packages consistent in size.

We simply press the sausage mix into a plastic bowl, usually a recycled whipped topping bowl, which makes up about one pound to one and half pounds, and then place it into the bag, either freezer or vacuum-pack. Sausage may also be formed into loaves or rolls and baked. Regardless, unless the sausage is to be smoked, or cooked later, you may wish to fry up a bit to taste your mix before freezing. This is where you can really enjoy your work.

SAUSAGE CASINGS

Many sausages are stuffed into casings to hold the ground meat in shape while it is cooked or smoked and also to determine the size and shape of the different sausages. Casings must be strong enough to hold the meat, yet pliable enough to allow for contraction and expansion during stuffing and cooking or smoking. Casings are available in several forms—natural, edible synthetic, synthetic/fibrous, cloth, and plastic.

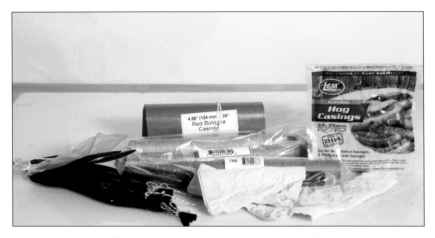

Many sausages are stuffed into casings, which are available in several forms and sizes.

Natural casings from sheep, hogs, and cattle, such as those used with these brats, are traditional and available in a number of shapes.

Natural casings, the traditional form, are edible, are permeable to water vapor and smoke, and have been used since the earliest days of sausage making. Natural casings are made from the cleaned intestines of animals, including sheep, hog, and beef casings. The inner lining is removed and the outer submucosa layer of collagen utilized. These casings are available in a wide range of sizes, depending on the source. Sheep casings are about ¾ in. in diameter and are commonly used in fresh breakfast sausage to create links or for frankfurters. Hog casings come in several different sizes and are the most commonly used. Hog casings are usually about 1 in. in diameter but can be obtained in larger sizes and are used for Italian sausage, pepperoni, and large frankfurters and hot dogs. Other less commonly used hog casings include hog bungs and hog bladders, used for liver sausage and head cheese.

Beef casings are used for cooked and smoked sausages, such as salami, bologna, Polish sausage, and others. The most commonly used beef casings are beef rounds and middles. Other beef casing products include beef bungs, used for large bologna; beef bladders, used for round Mortadella; and beef rounds, used for ring bologna, ring liver sausage, and others. Usually recipes will recommend the size of casings to be used. Some beef casings are rather tough and are commonly peeled away before the product is consumed.

Most of the common natural casings, except bungs, bladders, and so forth, are sold in lengths, usually of

Natural casings are packed in salt and must first be prepared for use by soaking in cold water.

Open one end of the casing and flush water through the casing. Keep the casings in cold water until use.

Edible synthetic or collagen casings are also available in several sizes and do not require as much preparation as natural casings.

several feet, called "hanks," or they are sold in bulk, in yards. A hank (or small container), around 60 feet of hog casings, will normally stuff from forty to fifty pounds of sausage.

Natural casings are packed in salt and must be prepared at least two to three hours before use. Remove the casings from the packing and cut into 3 or 4 ft. lengths for ease of handling. Rinse in cold water to remove the salt. Using two fingers inserted into one end of the casing, open the casing end and hold under running water to flush the casing. Pinch off the ends and shake the water around in the casing a bit. Check for any leaks indicating breaks. Next, place the casing in a bowl of water and soak for two to three hours. Changing the water after the first hour also helps.

If you must hold the casings for a short time, add a bit of vinegar to the water. Make sure the casings are wet before placing on the stuffing horn. Tough casings are usually caused by not allowing them to soak thoroughly before use. Leftover casings should be drained of any water and repacked in salt in the original container. Stored in a refrigerator, they will keep for about a year.

Edible synthetic casings are made from collagen, derived from the protein found inside the hides of pigs or cattle. This ground material, processed into a bread-dough-like mass, is extruded through a die of the desired diameter. In commercial sausage making, the collagen and meat blend is coextruded and then the outside of the sausage is coated with vinegar to cause it to set up. Collagen casings have become quite common, mostly because they allow for more economical sausage production. They are available in the same basic sizes as natural casings but do not need as much prestuffing preparation.

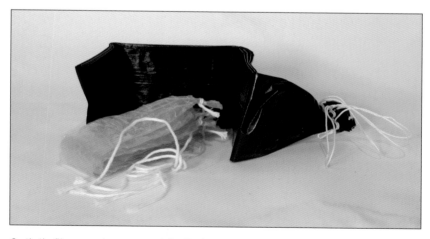

Synthetic fibrous casings are used for the larger sausages, and are peeled or cut off before consuming the sausage.

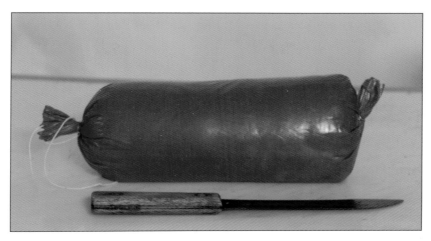

Nonedible, impermeable plastic casings are available for making skinless hot dogs or bologna.

These casings are also permeable to both water vapor and smoke. Both natural and collagen casings tend to have an odor when you first open the packet they are contained in; however, this odor dissipates fairly quickly and is nothing to be concerned about.

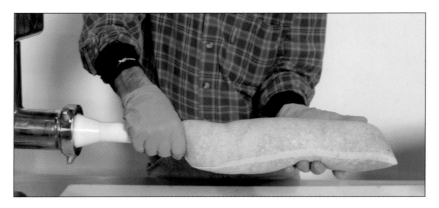

Cloth or muslin casings are also used for making many sausages.

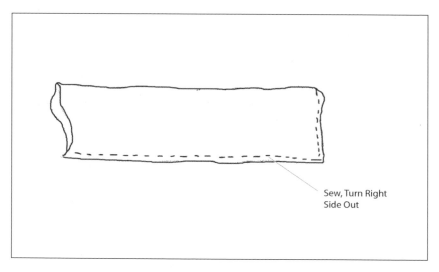

Sew, Turn Right
Side Out

Muslin casings can easily be sewn at home.

Synthetic fibrous casings are also often used for sausages that will be sliced, such as summer sausage, bologna, and so forth. In smaller sizes, the synthetic fibrous casings are used to produce "skinless" wieners and franks. After cooking the casings are skinned off. These fibrous casings are also available for larger sausages and are commonly used for salami and summer sausage. They are not edible but packaged dry and ready for use. They often come with one end tied closed. If you want a smoked flavor, synthetic casings are available with smoke flavor added to the inside of the casings. The casings are available in different colors, and you can also get fibrous casings with deer heads stamped on them, identifying deer or wild game sausage. Fibrous casings are available in sizes from ¾ in. to 6 in. in diameter and can be used for a wide variety of sausages.

Impermeable plastic casings are also available. These casings are not edible and must be peeled off before eating. They are most commonly used for hot dogs or bologna.

Cloth or muslin casings have traditionally been used as well. Our family has used these homemade casings for stuffing fresh breakfast sausage for many years. The

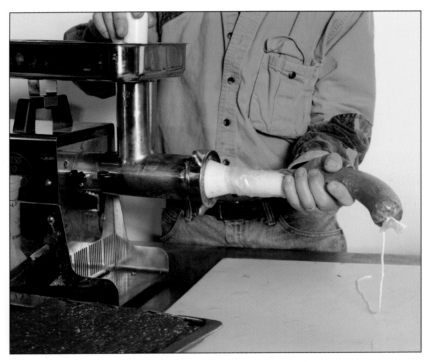

You really begin to feel like a sausage maker when you're stuffing sausage, which can be done in several ways. One of the easiest ways is to stuff at the same time you grind, using a grinder with a stuffing attachment.

sausage is hand-stuffed into the casings and the rolls and then frozen. To cook the sausage rolls, slice them to create patties, remove the muslin, and then fry the shaped patties.

Muslin casings are sewn into the sizes needed. For breakfast sausage we create sewn casings that are 2 in. in diameter and about 16 in. long. To make the casings, sew 5×18 in. strips of folded-over muslin into "tubes." Muslin casings should be soaked in water and then wrung out before using, or they will dry the sausage as it is stuffed into them. I also use these casings for making venison summer sausage.

STUFFING SAUSAGES

Stuffing is where the fun comes in—when you feel like you're really making sausage. Stuffing may be done by hand, with handheld stuffers, with stuffing tubes attached to meat grinders, or with some food processors. My mom hand-stuffed our breakfast sausage into muslin tubes, as we didn't have a sausage stuffer. I remember it was a fairly long and difficult process. When I began to make summer sausage from deer meat many years ago, I used a very primitive hand stuffer. It consisted of a tube with a stuffing tube on one end and a plunger pushed in by hand. It also was a lot of work. Then I acquired a 3-pound lever-operated stuffer from The Sausage Maker, Inc., and it made stuffing much easier. A better choice is a gear-driven, hand-cranked stuffer, such as the LEM model

You can also stuff using a plunger-operated stuffer. Make sure the stuffer is solidly fastened to a work surface. I fasten the stuffer to a board that is then clamped to the work surface.

shown, and the ultimate is a quality grinder with stuffing attachment.

Make sure you have everything on hand before you begin stuffing. Meat should be chilled to below 40°F or slightly frozen before stuffing. The quicker you can stuff, the better. The first step is to choose the casing size and type desired for the specific sausage, then match the stuffing tube to the sausage size. Make sure the stuffer is solidly affixed to a large, cleanable work surface, as the cased sausage will be extruded out onto this surface. One method I've used is to screw the stuffer to a ¾ in. wooden board and clamp the board with the stuffer to a table or countertop with C-clamps.

A gear-driven, hand-cranked stuffer can process a lot of sausage in a short time. Make sure you match the stuffing tubes to the size of casings being used and the type of sausage being made.

Sausage can be ground and then stuffed, or stuffed at the same time it is ground, depending on the type of sausage and the equipment you have available. Regardless of the method used, sausage ingredients should be ground as soon as you get them mixed. Some older recipes call for letting the mix sit for a certain length of time, usually overnight, so the ingredients can blend together. All this does is allow the salt in the cure and seasonings to set up the sausage, making it almost impossible to stuff. The ingredients will blend just as well in the casings. Adding one ounce of water per pound of meat during the mixing process will also help make stuffing easier. This allows the meat to flow easier from the stuffer, filling the casings more uniformly. Water will not weaken the flavor of your sausage.

If you have purchased a new stuffer, read the instructions for your particular stuffer. If you've purchased or inherited an older-model hand stuffer, the steps are basically the same, regardless of the model or type.

Regardless of what type of hand stuffer you have, make sure you pack the meat tightly into the stuffer to avoid air spaces, as air will be pushed into the casing during the stuffing process. Turn the handle or push down the lever until the meat shows in the end of the stuffing tube. Again,

It's important to make sure the meat is well packed into the stuffer to eliminate air pockets.

make sure the casings are washed, flushed, or soaked, depending on the type used. Lubricate the "horn" or tube of the stuffer. Use water for natural casings, cooking oil for collagen casings. If making fresh sausage, brats, or other sausages using natural or collagen casings, slide the casing all the way onto the stuffing tube. Pull about two inches of casing from the tube and tie the end in a knot. Push the tied end back against the stuffing tube. This will prevent air from being trapped in the casing.

Holding the casing in place on the stuffing tube with one hand, turn the handle or push the lever with the other hand and fill the casing. Do so gently at first, until the sausage begins to fill the casing. As the sausage comes out of the tube, it will pull the casing off the tube. Allow

Lubricate the horn of the stuffer with water for natural casings, or use spray cooking oil for collagen casings. Slide the casing all the way onto the horn of the stuffer and tie a knot in the end.

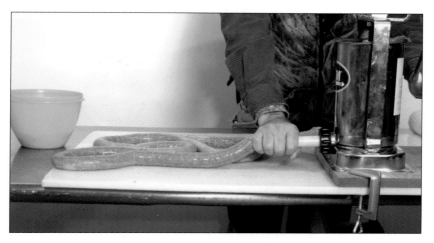

Holding the casing in place, turn the handle or push the plunger to fill the casings. As the sausage feeds into the casing, it will force the casing off the horn. If air pockets form, prick with a pin or toothpick.

the stuffed casings to feed out onto a large surface in front of the stuffer.

Although stuffing sausage isn't particularly hard to do, it takes a bit of practice to learn how full to stuff the casings. Two people definitely make the chore easier. If making sausages into links, it's important to not overstuff the casing. Casings will usually have some air pockets during filling. Using a sharp item such as a pin or toothpick, prick the casing to allow the air to escape. If you don't do this, the casing will burst at these locations during cooking or leave air pockets to collect mold in sausages such as summer sausage.

If the sausage is to be made into links and you are using natural casings, twist the stuffed casing into 4 to 6 in. links. Simply twist four to six times to create the links.

When using natural casings, twist the casings into links.

Some makers prefer to twist all in the same direction and then, after drying or smoking, they will use a sharp knife to cut through the twisted areas to separate into individual links. If using collagen casings, you will need to tie off the links, as collagen will unwind. Use cotton butcher's string tied tightly in place. Make two ties at each link space, and

Collagen and plastic casings require you to tie off the links with butcher's string.

Fibrous casing ends are often closed with hog rings and a hog ringer.

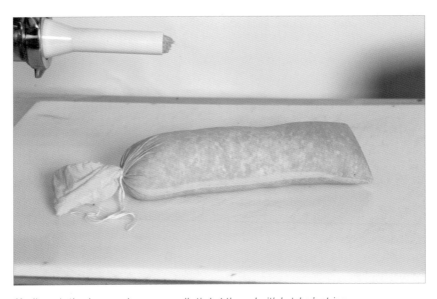

Muslin and other large casings are usually tied at the end with butcher's string.

then cut between the ties with a sharp knife. If making a sausage such as bologna "rounds," simply tie off at the end of the casing.

If making summer sausage or others from fibrous casings, again, soak the casings in warm water for twenty to thirty minutes before using. Follow the recipe directions for mixing the ingredients, but make sure you do not overmix. Mix only until the meat feels tacky and then stuff immediately. Again, fill the stuffer with meat and pack it thoroughly in place. Turn the handle or push down the plunger until the meat begins to show at the end of the stuffing tube.

Fibrous casings usually have one end tied, or clipped, shut. Slide the fibrous casing all the way on the stuffing tube. Then hold the fibrous casing securely back in place on the stuffing tube and use the plunger or handle to force the sausage into the casing. Go gently, and make sure the tied end is tight against the stuffing tube when you begin to prevent adding air into the end of the casing. If air pockets develop, prick with a sharp object. Fill the casing to approximately one and half inches from the end. Twist the end of the casing tightly and tie with cotton butcher's string or fasten with "hog rings" and a hog-ringer tool.

In either case, if you run out of sausage before completely filling the casing, simply leave casing in place and refill the stuffer. There will always be a remainder of sausage in the tube. If you run out of casings before sausage, simply add another casing.

CHAPTER 5

Smoking and Cooking Sausages

Many sausages are cold-smoked, either to dry or to add flavor. Other sausages are smoke-cooked to help preserve them. Many sausages are also cooked by other means, such as in an oven, by steaming, or by simmering in water. Whatever the method, all sausages must be heated to an internal temperature of 160°F (165°F for sausages containing poultry) at some point before they are consumed.

Many sausages are cold-smoked to add flavor. They may also be smoke/cooked or cooked using other methods. Regardless, all sausages must be heated to an internal temperature of 160° F. (165° F for those containing poultry) before consuming. The Masterbuilt Electric Digital Smokehouse makes this task easy.

SMOKING

You will, of course, need a means of smoking, as described in chapter 2. There are different levels of smoking—cold-smoking, smoke-cooking, and barbecuing or hot-smoking. The latter also has some variance but for the most part means cooking meats, with or without smoke, at 200° to 350°F. The latter is commonly called barbecuing or grilling because it's usually done on a grill, but it can also be done in a charcoal or electric smoker. Barbecuing or grilling is not typically the type of smoking used for making sausages.

Regardless of the method used, smoking meat adds flavor. The amount of flavor depends on the length of smoking time, as well as the density of smoke and the type of material, usually wood chips, used for smoking. In cold-smoking, the smoke is used to dry out the sausage and add flavor. In this case the temperature is usually kept below 130°F, as the proteins in meat start to become cooked at higher than 130°F. The cold-smoked, finished sausage, however, must still be considered "raw," since it has not been heat-treated to 160°F. The sausage must be cooked to 160°F internal temperature before consuming.

Some fermented dry sausages, such as traditional pepperoni, are the exception. These are traditionally dried and smoked but not cooked. Many smoked sausages also utilize a curing agent before smoking. The process of curing utilizes salt and other curing agents to bring about certain physical and chemical changes that have the effect of stabilizing the meat and also act to suppress the growth of bacteria.

Smoking sausages consists of three steps: 1) drying the sausage before smoking, 2) smoking, and 3) after-smoke handling. Each step is important not only for the taste but also for the appearance of the sausage. After all, you want your sausage to look great as well as taste great.

DRYING

Properly drying sausage gives it that nice, browned appearance, especially important in link sausage or those using natural or collagen casings. The sausage should be dry to the touch before you begin smoking; however, they shouldn't be overly dried for too long a period. When they are dry to the touch, they are sufficiently dry. Some sausages, such as traditional salami, are simply dried, rather than being cooked. Again, refer to the section in chapter 3 regarding the dangers of drying without heat treatment.

Sausage can be dried in two ways: 1) natural air-drying, or 2) with produced heat, such as in a smoker. Air-drying is the simplest, but it requires the correct conditions. Sausage drying should be done in cool weather. The ideal weather is 40° to 50°F or less, but not below freezing, and with a relative humidity of 70 to 80 percent. Air-drying can be done as long as the humidity isn't too high. You can air-dry in a cardboard box, in the shade on sunny days, so long as you ensure that the sausages are protected from

Smoking can be used to add flavor or to cook sausages.

insects and varmints. You don't want the neighborhood cat or dog to consume the product of all your hard work.

Regardless of where the sausages are to be dried, it's important that they be supported properly. They can be hung on wooden dowels or smokehouse sticks, or they can be placed on racks. Laying the sausages on racks will alter the shape and appearance somewhat. You can create simple hanging racks for air-drying. Make sure the sausages do not touch each other during the drying

Sausages to be smoked should first be dried to the touch to have a nice, even, brown appearance without blotches. Air-drying is one method.

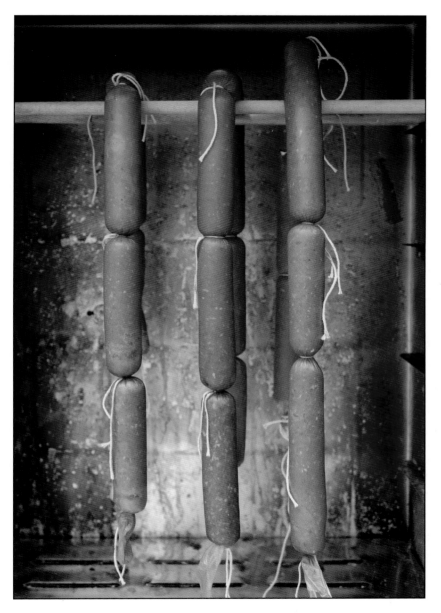

Sausages can also be air-dried in a smoker. Set the smoker to low with the damper open, and do not use smoke.

process. It's important for the air to circulate evenly around each sausage; if this doesn't happen, damp spots or areas will turn white after the smoking process. You can also use a small fan, set on a low speed, to help circulate air around the sausages. There is no set timetable for drying sausages. The time will depend on the ambient temperature, humidity, and how they are dried.

Sausages can also be dried in a smoker. This is actually the easiest method, but the smoker must have some kind of temperature control. Simply set the smoker to low (below 90°F) and allow the sausages to dry to the touch. Don't overheat the sausages, and don't add smoke at this point. If you use too high a temperature, the sausages will never get dry but will sweat and start to cook. A high temperature will also make the casings tough. If you have a home-made smoker with an electric hot plate or other heating element, it can be used, without wood chips, to help dry out the sausages, and a small fan inside the smoker can help circulate air. Once the sausages are dry to the touch, simply increase the heat.

SMOKING

The actual process of smoking is both an art and a skill. Too much smoke, and your product will taste bitter; too little smoke, and no flavor is added. Experience with your particular smoker is the best teacher. Part of the fun of making and smoking sausages is the learning experience. You may get to enjoy several "mistakes" before perfecting your recipes and smoking techniques.

Smoking requires wood of some sort—chips, sawdust, or compressed wood materials, depending on the type of smoker used. The chips are placed in the smoker, according to the manufacturer's instructions.

The Bradley Electric Smoker uses compressed chips fed automatically into the smoker.

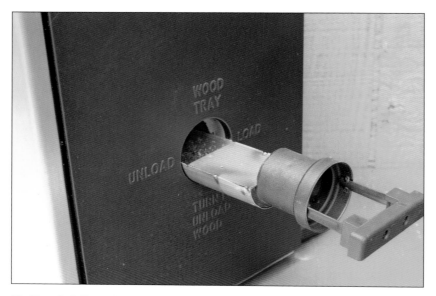

The Masterbuilt Electric Digital Smokehouse has an externally fed chip pan to hold the chips.

Smoking requires some sort of material to create the smoke. The most common materials are wood chips, wood sawdust, or compressed pellets of wood materials. The type of wood used determines the flavor, with some woods providing a more flavorful smoke than others. Hickory is one of the strongest and most common types of wood used for smoking. Fruitwoods, such as apple, peach, and pear, provide a nice flavor. Mesquite, alder, maple, and pecan are also good choices. Do not use resinous woods such as pine or fir, as they produce resins and a bitter, off taste.

Pellets designed for specific smokers should be used according to the manufacturer's instructions. Sawdust and chips are usually placed in a chip pan. They should be soaked in water for an hour or so, and the water then

If the smoke is to be used for flavor only (and not as a means of cooking), it is called cold-smoking, or heating at no more than 130° F. The Bradley Electric Smoker has an accessory made for cold-smoking.

drained off. Another old-fashioned smoking material is corncobs, which produce a good smoke.

The smoker is fired up and preheated a bit, depending on whether you have a wood-fueled fire or an electric smoker. The sausages are suspended in the smoker, if they are not already in place from the drying process. The soaked chips and chip pan is placed in the smoker and the dampers closed.

The process of smoking sausages is basically cold-smoking, and the meat is then thermal-treated. Different sausages require different smoker temperature ranges for their processes. In most instances, however, it's important to not allow the temperature to rise above 130°F for the smoking process. If the meat is smoked at high temperatures, the fat will be forced out of the casings. You will lose some fat during the smoking and cooking stages, but

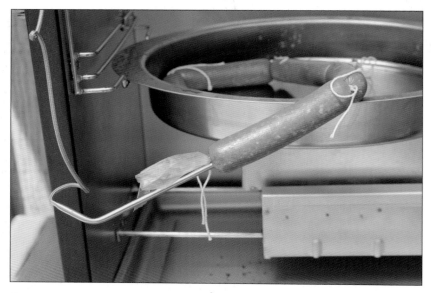

Sausages may also be heat-treated or cooked in the smoker. Simply raise the temperature to cook until the internal temperature of the sausages reaches 160°F. The Masterbuilt Electric Digital Smokehouse shown here includes a meat probe.

some fat content is important to bind the meat particles together.

As you can guess, an electric-heated smoker with temperature controls makes the task easier, but you can also regulate a wood-fired smoker by controlling the amount of fire in the firebox using the dampers. A wood-fired smoker just doesn't react as quickly and takes a bit more patience.

Again, you want smoke flavor, but not too much. Depending on the type of wood and the sausages being smoked, the smoking time will vary. With the lighter-smoking fruitwoods, such as apple, or woods such as pecan or mesquite, this usually will be from four to five hours.

Some sausages can simply be baked in an oven.

A steamer can also be made to cook sausages, or sausages can be simmered or poached in hot water to an internal temperature of 160° F.

The smoke from stronger-flavored woods, such as hickory, is often stopped after about three to four hours. Stopping usually means simply not replenishing the wood chips.

In many instances the sausages are then heated in the smoker for the heat treatment. Simply remove the smoke materials and continue the heat process. In this case the temperature inside the smoker is usually increased, sometimes in incremental stages. The timing and temperature depends on the sausage being made. Regardless, the sausage should be cooked to an internal temperature of 160°F, and some commercial mixes suggest 165°F. Any sausages containing poultry should always be heated to 165°F.

Regardless of whether they are smoked, sausages may be heat-treated to 160°F in other ways, as well. The first is to simply bake the sausages in an oven. This is the only choice for some sausage loaves. Oven baking can also be used when sausages, such as summer sausage and others, are not stuffed but simply rolled into logs. In this case the sausages are placed on a rack above a shallow pan or cookie sheet and baked at 325°F, until the internal temperature reaches 160°F.

Another method is to steam-cook the sausages, using a steamer created from a large pan with an elevated rack inside and a lid to cover. After cold-smoking (if desired for flavor), wrap each sausage in plastic food wrap and steam until the internal temperature reaches 160°F.

Many of the German and Polish sausages, such as liver sausage, bologna, and frankfurters, are simmered in water for the heat treatment, regardless of whether they have been smoked. The sausages should be simmered in 180°F water until the internal temperature reaches 160°F. Do not place cold sausages into simmering water, as they will burst immediately. Place in warm water and then bring the water to simmering. Depending on the type and size of the sausages, this can take from fifteen minutes to an hour. A thermometer with a remote temperature probe makes this task easier.

HANDLING AFTER SMOKING/COOKING

One of the most important steps in creating not only good-tasting but good-looking sausages is how they are

Regardless of the thermal-heating method used, the sausages must be immediately cooled. This can be done with cold water from a garden hose or by one of the easiest methods: immediately plunging the sausages into a sink, large tub, or cooler filled with ice water, adding ice as needed.

Allow the sausages to air-dry for an hour or two to add the "bloom," or finished appearance.

handled after the smoking and heat treatment. Actually, two steps are required for this phase.

Immediately after the smoking/cooking phase, the sausages must be cooled down quickly or they will shrink up and the casings will shrivel. This phase is called "showering" and must be done immediately. Showering can be done in two ways. For small batches of sausage, simply immerse them immediately in ice water in a large tub, a pan, or your kitchen sink.

Another method—for larger batches of sausage—is to spray them with cold water from a garden hose. In this case, you'll need a rack ready to hold the sausages, near the smoker. The sausages should be cooled down to 100° to 110°F as quickly as possible. If you're a bit slow and the sausages shrink and shrivel, place them back in a 180°F water bath to replump them, and then shower them off again. This will work to some degree (although the sausages won't be quite as plump as they would have been had the process been done properly the first time).

The final step is to add the "bloom" to your sausages. This means simply allowing them to age by air-drying. Blooming will usually require from two to four hours, depending on the type of sausage and the casing used. Simply hang the sausages back in the smoker (with no heat), or place them in a shady, fairly cool spot with lots of air circulation. If you made a rack for showering them, you can also use it for blooming.

With the correct drying, smoking, and/or heat treatment, you should have plump, well-browned sausages.

The sausages should be eaten immediately or stored in the refrigerator for three to four days. Sausages that will not be consumed immediately should be frozen. Vacuum-packing will help them keep for up to nine or ten months in your freezer.

CHAPTER 6

Fresh Sausage

One of my favorite butchering-day memories is of the first "test" batch of fresh pork sausage fried up in a big iron skillet—so fresh, in fact, that it had just been ground moments before. Nothing can compare with this taste. And it's the way my family determined whether to add more or less of some ingredients—salt or spices, such as more red pepper. Fresh sausage is a tradition in many countries. In most instances, fresh sausage is made of pork, but other meats may be added as well, including venison, lamb, or mutton. In this case, the proportions are usually two parts lamb or mutton to one part pork, or three parts venison to two parts pork. Beef and pork combined in varying amounts are another common fresh sausage mixture.

Fresh sausage (such as breakfast sausage) is some of the simplest to make and is often made into patties.

Fresh sausage is just that—fresh, not cured—and it must be consumed immediately, refrigerated for a short time, or frozen for future use. Since these sausage recipes are all "fresh," the amount of salt in each can be reduced to taste because the salt is not part of a curing process. In the past, fresh sausage was often made into patties, fried, then placed in stone crocks and covered with melted lard. Not particularly tasty, and not government safe, but essential in those days.

Fresh sausage is popular the world over and is made hundreds of different ways, using a wide variety of recipes. The following are some of the more-popular fresh sausages we like. You can vary the seasonings to have the fun of creating your own sausage recipes. Who knows—they might be handed down through your family, as have many of the following recipes.

Burch Pork Sausage
10 lbs. pork trimmings from butchering
¼ cup coarse or canning salt
⅛ cup black pepper
½ to 1 tbsp. crushed red pepper

We keep this basic sausage mix fairly lean, without adding additional fat, and use only basic salt and pepper flavorings. You can also add a bit of ground cayenne pepper instead of, or in addition to, the crushed red pepper. We grow our own cayenne peppers just for this recipe. This sausage has a really rich, meaty taste that is equally good for breakfast or a sausage burger.

Spread the cut chunks of meat out on a work surface and sprinkle the salt and peppers over the meat. Run the seasoned meat through a grinder using a ⅛ in. plate. In the past, we stuffed the sausage into muslin casings and froze the extra. To use, simply slice the muslin-cased sausages into half-inch-thick patties. We've also simply made the meat into patties and frozen with waxed paper between each patty. The sausage can be stuffed into sheep casings for breakfast-link sausages and can also be smoked. Consume immediately or freeze for later use.

Morton Salt Breakfast Sausage

10 lbs. boneless pork trimmings ($^2/_3$ to ¾ lean)

½ cup plus 2 tbsps. Morton Sausage and Meat Loaf Seasoning Mix

Natural casings, rinsed and drained (optional)

(Note: For smaller quantities, use 1 tbsp. Morton Sausage and Meat Loaf Seasoning Mix per pound of pork trimmings or ground pork.)

This is a very tasty and easy sausage. Cut meat and fat into 1 in. cubes. Thoroughly mix meat, fat, and seasonings. Grind through coarse plate of meat grinder. Refrigerate sausage overnight before making into patties.

Most breakfast sausage recipes are fairly simple, but prepared mixes are also available. In most instances the meat is cut into small squares or strips, the spices are sprinkled over the meat, and then the meat is ground.

The sausage may also be stuffed into casings. If you are stuffing the sausage into casings, do not refrigerate it first. Consume immediately or freeze for later use.

To pan-fry: Place links or patties into a cold, ungreased skillet. Fry slowly until well browned and thoroughly cooked.

To bake: Place sausages in a single layer in a shallow baking pan. Bake at 400°F, turning occasionally until done, about twenty to thirty minutes.

Farm-Fresh Breakfast Sausage
5 lbs 100 percent Boston butt pork
2 tbsps. coarse canning or meat salt
2 tsps. ground black pepper

Breakfast sausage may also be stuffed into sheep casings for links or into muslin bags for slicing into patties.

2 tsps. rubbed sage

½ tsp. ginger

1 tsp. thyme

1 tsp. nutmeg

2 tsps. crushed red pepper

1 tbsp. brown sugar

If you like a spicy flavored breakfast sausage, this is a good choice. Pure pork butt provides a really meaty, lean sausage. You can substitute 50 percent pork butt and 50 percent trimmings for a less-lean sausage. Cut the meat into 1-inch chunks. Mix the spices well in a bowl and sprinkle over the cut meat. Mix the spices and meat together and then grind through a ⅛ in. plate. Make

Making your own brown-and-serve sausage is easy. We like to use this method with maple-flavored sausage, which is great for serving with pancakes. Ingredients include brown sugar and maple flavoring.

Mix all ingredients together, spread over the cut meat, and mix well.

into patties or stuff into lamb or hog casings for links or muslin bags or 2 ½ in. fibrous casings for slicing. This sausage must be cooked before consuming. Freeze any sausage not consumed immediately.

One method we've used is to extrude sausage through a "jerky gun" to create brown-and-serve "links." First, fill the gun with ground meat.

Western Breakfast Sausage

5 lbs. pork butt

2 tbsps. salt

1 tbsp. black pepper

1 tbsp. chili powder

1 tsp. garlic powder

½ tsp. marjoram

½ tsp. coriander

Pinch of thyme

1 tsp. crushed red pepper

Next, extrude the maple-flavored sausage out onto cookie sheets or flat pans, lined with butcher paper (waxed side up).

This sausage has even more spice and flavor. If you prefer a less-hot version, do not add the red pepper, or cut back on the black pepper or chili powder.

Cut the meat into 1 in. chunks. Mix the spices well in a bowl and sprinkle over the cut meat. Mix the spices and meat together and then grind through a ⅛ in. plate. Make into patties or stuff into lamb or hog casings for links or a muslin bag or 2 ½ in. fibrous casings for slicing. This sausage must be cooked before consuming. Freeze any sausage not consumed immediately.

Bake in a 325°F oven until thoroughly cooked, and then cut into links. Microwave to heat and then serve.

Maple-Flavored Sausage

6 lbs. pork butt or pork trimmings

3 tbsps. coarse or canning salt

4 heaping tbsps. brown sugar

1 tbsp. ground black pepper

1 tsp. crushed red pepper

½ tsp. maple flavoring

Maple-flavored pork sausage and pancakes or waffles go hand in hand. And when you make the sausage brown-and-serve (see Brown-and-Serve Breakfast Sausage Links or Patties, below), you have an almost instant tasty breakfast you and your family or guests will really enjoy.

Cut the meat into 1 in. chunks. Mix the spices well in a bowl and sprinkle over the cut meat. Mix the spices and meat together and then grind through a ⅛ in. plate. Make into patties or stuff into lamb or hog casings for links or into a muslin bag or 2 ½ in. fibrous casings for slicing. Use immediately or freeze for later use.

The LEM grinder also comes with a patty-maker accessory that will produce large quantities of patties quickly.

Tex-Mex Pork Sausage

5 lbs. lean pork butt

2 tbsps. coarse or canning salt

1 tbsp. ground black pepper

1 tbsp. garlic powder or 5 minced garlic cloves

1 tsp. ground cumin

1 tsp. ground coriander

1 tbsp. chili powder

2 tsps. ground chipotle pepper

Tex-Mex is a medium-hot sausage with a distinct Southwestern flavor. This is a great sausage to mix in with scrambled eggs for an unusual "cowboy" breakfast. You can add or subtract the peppers for more or less heat.

Cut the meat into 1 in. chunks. Mix the spices well in a bowl and sprinkle over the cut meat. Mix the spices and meat together and then grind through a $1/8$ in. plate. Make into patties or stuff into lamb or hog casings for links or a muslin bag or 3 ½ in. fibrous casings for slicing. This sausage must be cooked before consuming. Freeze any sausage not consumed immediately.

Whole-Hog Sausage

100 lbs. of deboned hog meat

2 lbs. coarse or canning salt

4 oz ground black pepper

1 oz thyme

1 oz ground ginger

1 oz ground nutmeg

½ oz dried marjoram
2 oz crushed red pepper

As we've discovered, whole-hog sausage is very popular for sausage and pancake breakfasts, which are great moneymakers for churches, civic groups, and other organizations. Of course, you may also wish to do up a whole hog and divide it among family and friends.

In the past, heavy hogs were often used for this type of sausage, but these days the best choice is a 200 to 250 lbs., fairly lean hog. Most folks simply have the butcher do this chore for them, butchering and making the sausage; that way, you have proven results, important when serving the sausage to the community. You can do the job yourself, but you'll need the help of friends, and the weather will have to be cold and stay cold until the sausage is consumed or in the freezer. It's extremely important to have all the ingredients and equipment ready, along with a cold place to work.

The best method is to cool down the hog overnight, immediately after butchering, and then work up the sausage the next day. One alternative we've used several times is to have the butcher do the killing, skinning, and cutting the hog into halves, then the butcher cools the carcass down overnight in his cooler. Regardless, after cooling the hog, debone the meat and discard any blood clots and excess fat. The ideal meat mixture should be about 75 percent lean meat and 25 percent fat. You may need to leave out some of the backfat to have the correct mixture.

Cut the meat into 1 in. chunks, weigh, and mix in the spices with the meat chunks in big tubs. Then grind through a $1/8$ in. or $3/16$ in. plate. Remix the meat to make sure the spices are evenly distributed, and then cool overnight in large tubs in a cooler or refrigerator. Consume immediately or freeze until the event or for future use. In most instances, whole-hog sausage is made into patties before cooking, an event often called a "patty pig." A patty maker is a great helpmate for this chore.

Brown-and-Serve Breakfast Sausage Links or Patties

Follow any of the fresh pork breakfast sausage recipes above and extrude into links or make into patties and bake. When we were doing our jerky book, we experimented with squeezing the sausage meat through a jerky gun. Voilà—instant sausage links, without having to stuff the sausages. Extrude the sausage links onto the waxed side of freezer paper that is placed on cookie sheets, or make sausage patties and place on the waxed side of freezer paper–lined cookie sheets. Bake in a 350° oven until thoroughly cooked. Then simply cut into the lengths desired (or the number of patties desired) and freeze in vacuum-sealed packages.

To cook, place the frozen links or patties on a microwaveable plate and microwave until heated through. The sausage links or patties can also be heated in a skillet on top of the stove or in the oven.

Fresh Sweet Italian Sausage

5 lbs. pork butt or lean pork trimmings

1 tbsp. brown sugar

2 tbsps. coarse or canning salt

1 tsp. coarse-ground black pepper

1½ tsps. cracked fennel seed

½ tsp. sweet basil

1 tbsp. garlic powder or 5 minced garlic cloves

½ tsp. oregano

1 tsp. paprika

1 cup water

Making your own brats is also fun and a great way to make your own barbecue party foods.

You can also get prepacked "kits" that include all the necessary spices for making sausages such as brats.

Fresh sweet Italian sausage can be used in any number of dishes. It's great to keep in your freezer for spicing up dishes. Cut meat into 1 in. chunks and then coarse-grind. Add the spices to the water. Pour over the meat and mix well, then place in flat pans and freeze for an hour or so to firm up the meat. Cut into 1 in. squares and re-grind through a fine plate. Stuff the sausage into pork or collagen casings. This sausage must be cooked before consuming. Consume immediately or freeze. In many instances this sausage is not smoked, but you can add the smoked flavor by cold-smoking.

Hot Italian Sausage

5 lbs. pork trimmings

2 tbsps. coarse or canning salt

1 tbsp. coarse-ground black pepper

5 tsps. cracked fennel seed

1 cup chopped fresh parsley

Some fresh sausages such as brats or Italian sausage are stuffed into natural collagen casings.

1 tbsp. garlic powder or 5 minced garlic cloves
½ tsp. caraway seeds
3 tbsps. paprika
1 tbsp. ground red pepper
2 tsps. crushed red pepper
1 cup dry red wine

A quite hot and spicy sausage, it tastes great on pizzas. You can actually make this as hot as you desire or less hot by adding or subtracting the amount of hot peppers you use. Cut meat into 1 in. chunks and then coarse-grind. Add the seasonings into the wine and pour over the meat. Mix well, then place in flat pans and freeze for an hour or so to firm up the meat. Cut the frozen chunks into 1 in. squares and re-grind through a fine plate. Stuff the sausage into pork or collagen casings. This sausage must be cooked before consuming and must be consumed immediately or frozen.

In most instances this sausage is not smoked but served fresh. You can add the smoked flavor by cold-smoking. Place in a smoker preheated to 140°F, dry for about an hour, and then smoke until you achieve the desired color.

To cook the sausage, raise the temperature to 180°F and cook until the internal temperature reaches 160°F. This sausage is then considered "cooked" and is ready to eat, but it must still be kept refrigerated or frozen.

Bratwurst

3 lbs. pork butt

2 lbs. veal (or substitute 2 pounds of venison)

1 cup milk

2 eggs

2 tbsps. coarse or canning salt

2 tsps. ground white or black pepper

1½ tsps. mace

1 tsp. ground nutmeg

½ tsp. ground ginger

1 cup soy protein concentrate

Bratwurst is a fun and easy sausage to make. It can be grilled or cooked in a variety of dishes. Cut meat into 1 in. chunks and then coarse-grind. Add the soy concentrate and seasonings to the milk and beaten eggs. Mix well into the ground meat. Place the ground, spiced mixture in flat pans and freeze for an hour or so to firm up the meat. Cut the frozen meat into 1 in. squares and re-grind through a fine plate. For finer "brats," refreeze and re-grind. Stuff the sausage into pork or collagen casings.

Bratwurst is actually produced in three types: fresh, cooked, or smoked. If you use it fresh, cook and consume it immediately or freeze. To cook, place it in a cooker and steam at 180°F until the internal temperature of 160°F is reached. To smoke, place it in a preheated smoker at 120°F with no smoke and the damper open. Allow to dry until the casings are dry to the touch. Gradually increase the temperature to 180°F and add wood chips. Hold at that temperature until the internal temperature of the sausage reaches 160°F. Remove and shower with cold water to cool and then allow the sausages to dry. Whether fresh, cooked, or smoked, this sausage must be consumed immediately or frozen for later use.

Polish Sausage

3 lbs. ground pork trimmings
2 lbs. ground beef or ground venison
2 tsps. ground black pepper
2 tbsps. coarse or canning salt
1 tbsp. marjoram
1 tbsp. garlic powder or 5 minced garlic cloves
½ tsp. cayenne pepper
1 tblsp. sugar
1 cup ice water
½ tsp. caraway seeds

Polish sausage is another great "add-to" sausage for a variety of dishes. It is also great grilled and served on a bun. Cut meat into 1 in. chunks, then coarse-grind. Stir the spices in the water, spread evenly over the meat, and mix well. Place in flat pans and freeze for an hour or so to firm up the meat. Then cut into 1 in. squares and re-grind through a fine plate. Stuff the sausage into pork or collagen casings. This sausage must be cooked before consuming and must be consumed immediately or frozen for later use. In most instances this is not smoked, but you can add the smoked flavor by cold-smoking.

Cajun Hot Sausage
5 lbs. pork butt
5 tsps. coarse or canning salt
2 tbsps. coarse-ground black pepper
2 tsps. crushed red pepper
2 tsps. ground chili pepper
1 tbsp. garlic powder or 5 minced garlic cloves
1 tsp. onion powder
½ tsp. allspice
2 tsps. thyme
1 cup ice water

If you like Cajun foods you'll love this hot, spicy sausage added to any number of Cajun dishes, including gumbo. Cut meat into 1 in. chunks, then coarse-grind. Stir the spices into the water. Spread evenly over the meat and mix well. Then place in flat pans and freeze for an hour or so to firm up the meat. Cut into 1 in. squares and re-grind through a fine plate. Stuff the sausage into pork or collagen casings. This sausage must be cooked before consuming and must be consumed immediately or frozen for later use. In most instances this sausage is not smoked, but you can add the smoked flavor by cold-smoking.

Venison Breakfast Sausage

2 ½ lbs. venison
2 ½ lbs. fatty ground pork trimmings
2 tbsps. coarse or canning salt
1 ½ tsps. liquid smoke
1 tsp. garlic powder
1 tsp. onion powder
1 tsp. ground black pepper
1 cup ice water

A great way of serving deer for breakfast is to mix venison with pork. This sausage is made of fresh venison, and everyone in your deer camp will love it. Cut the meat into 1 in. chunks. Mix the spices and water well in a bowl and sprinkle over the cut meat. Mix the spices and meat well together, then grind through a ⅛ in. plate. Make into patties or stuff into lamb or hog casings for links or muslin bags or 3 ½ in. fibrous casings for slicing. This sausage must be cooked before consuming. Freeze any sausage not consumed immediately.

Wild Game Breakfast Sausage

3 lbs. of any type of game meat or fowl, even a mixture
2 lbs. fatty pork trimmings
2 tbsps. coarse or canning salt
1 tbsp. coarse-ground black pepper
1 tsp. ginger
1 tbsp. rubbed sage
1 tbsp. crushed red pepper
1 tbsp. garlic powder or 5 minced garlic cloves

This sausage is a great way to clean out your freezer of leftover game meat. Small game, waterfowl, big game—it can all be used, and each will add its own distinct flavor.

Cut the meat into 1 in. chunks. Stir the spices into the water and sprinkle over the cut meat. Evenly spread the spices over the meat and mix well together. Then grind through a ⅛ in. plate. Make into patties or stuff into lamb or hog casings for links or muslin bags or 2 ½ in. fibrous casings for slicing. This sausage must be cooked before consuming. Freeze any sausage not consumed immediately.

English Bangers
5 lbs. fatty pork trimmings
½ cup bread crumbs
2 tbsps. coarse or canning salt
1 tsp. ground black pepper
½ tsp. each of mace, sage, and ginger
1 cup cold water (or cold pork stock)

This sausage was popularized during World War II when meat was scarce, and many sausage makers added quite a bit of water to the recipe. These sausages often exploded when cooked because of the water and tight skin shrinking, giving them the name "bangers." This extremely popular breakfast sausage is often served with mashed potatoes, creating a national dish called "bangers and mash." Bangers are sometimes made with all beef trimmings, with 75 percent lean and 25 percent fat.

Cut the meat into 1 in. chunks. Blend the spices, bread crumbs, and water together and sprinkle evenly over the cut meat. Mix the spices and meat well together and then grind through a $^1/_8$ in. plate. Stuff into lamb or hog casings for links or muslin bags or 2 ½ in. fibrous casings for slicing. This sausage must be cooked before consuming. Freeze any sausage not consumed immediately.

CHAPTER 7

Dry, Semidry, and Hard Sausages

Hard sausages have been a tradition in many countries for centuries, primarily because some of them can be stored without refrigeration. Once cut into, however, these sausages will keep longer if refrigerated. A wide variety of hard sausages can be found. Most hard sausages today are not consumed at mealtime but used as snack or party foods. Some hard sausages may also be used in food preparation. These sausages were traditionally dried, not cooked, although cold-smoking was occasionally used to create flavor.

Because of the possibility of contracting trichinosis from the raw meat used for these uncooked sausages, freezing the meat before making the sausage is one safety precaution used by commercial producers. Freezing does not kill trichinosis in some animal meat, however, including bear, and it is also hard to do correctly at home.

These days, many of the traditionally "uncooked" sausages are thermal-heated, or cooked to an internal temperature of 160°F. One common method is smoke-cooking and then air-drying. All of these dry sausages also require the use of a curing agent, and some are also fermented.

Homemade traditional hard or dry sausages, such as summer sausage, make a great snack food to share with family and friends.

Freezing Sausages is a great way to store them until you're ready to eat.

Proper drying of these hard sausages also requires the right temperature and humidity. The ideal temperature is 45° to 50°F at about 70 to 80 percent humidity. At this temperature and humidity, it will take about sixty days to dry the sausages. This was traditionally done in the cold part of the year and, when done correctly, will remove about one-third of the weight of the sausage in moisture. The sausage will acquire some mold, but that can be washed off with a mild vinegar and water solution, or you can simply peel off the casing and mold before eating.

All of the semidry and hard sausages that are not dried must be refrigerated or frozen for future use. Dried sausages can be stored without refrigeration.

Venison summer sausage has become a favorite of ours, and we often make enough to give some away to friends and family. Summer sausage can also be made of other wild game meats, including waterfowl, as well as beef and mutton. Because of the popularity of this sausage, the nearly limitless number of ways it can be prepared, and the many recipes available, we've included recipes for several varieties.

Morton Salt Savory Summer Sausage

6 lbs. boneless pork trimmings
4 lbs. boneless beef trimmings
½ cup Morton Tender Quick Mix or Morton Sugar Cure (Plain) Mix
4 tbsps. liquid smoke
3 tbsps. sugar
1 tsp. ground black pepper
1 tsp. ground ginger
1 tsp. garlic powder

This Morton Salt version is an extremely easy recipe, especially if you don't have a sausage stuffer or smoker, and it's also a great "starter" sausage project. Cut meat into 1 in. cubes and mix with remaining ingredients. Grind through a ¼ in. plate. Refrigerate overnight.

Re-grind sausage through a ⅛ in. plate. Shape sausage into slender rolls, 8 to 10 ins. long and 1 ½ ins. in diameter. Wrap in plastic or foil. Refrigerate overnight.

Unwrap rolls and place on broiler pan. Bake at 325°F until a meat thermometer inserted in the center of the roll reads 160°F, about fifty to sixty minutes. Store wrapped in refrigerator. Use within three to five days, or freeze for later use.

Bradley Smoker Savory Summer Sausage

5 lbs. regular ground beef (not extra lean)

5 tsps. curing salt

3 ½ tsps. mustard seed

2 ½ tsps. coarse black pepper

½ tsp. garlic salt

1 cup water

Cooking oil spray

Most sausages use a combination of fat and lean meat. Grind fat separately.

Shown are bowls of ground pork fat and venison, ready to be made into sausage.

The Bradley Smoker folks offer this great recipe for use with their electric smokers. For simplicity, it uses purchased ground hamburger meat; however, venison or part venison could be used. In a large glass bowl, mix together all the ingredients by hand. Cover with plastic wrap and refrigerate for twenty-four hours, mixing twice during this time. Form the meat into five rolls, approximately 3 ins in diameter. Place the rolls on oiled smoker racks.

Preheat the Bradley Smoker to between 200° and 220°F. Place rolls on racks in the Bradley Smoker, and, using Bradley hickory-flavor bisquettes, smoke/ cook for approximately four to five hours until a meat thermometer reads 160° to 170°F.

To store, wrap in foil, put in plastic bags, and freeze. Take out an hour before serving, slice, and serve with cheese and crackers as an appetizer.

Venison Summer Sausage

3 lbs. venison, elk, or buffalo

2 lbs. pork trimmings

1 tbsp. black pepper

5 tbsps. Morton Tender Quick Mix or Morton Sugar Cure
(Plain) Mix

1 tsp. ground coriander

½ tsp. ground ginger

½ tsp. ground mustard

1 tsp. garlic powder

½ tsp. ground red pepper

4 tbsps. corn syrup

½ tsp. liquid smoke

Weigh meats separately. Cut chilled meat into 1 in.
cubes. Grind through a ³/₁₆ in. grinder plate. Thoroughly
mix ingredients in a glass bowl and pour over ground
meat. Mix meat and ingredients. Place in plastic or glass
bowl and refrigerate overnight.

Spread meat out to about 1 in. depth in a shallow, flat
pan and place in a freezer for an hour or so or until the
meat is partially frozen. Remove the partially frozen meat
and re-grind through a ⅛ in. plate. Stuff the ground meat
into synthetic casings. (If you have a meat grinder with
stuffing attachment, you can do this in one step.)

Hang the stuffed meat on drying racks and dry at
room temperature for four to five hours or place in a
smoker on sticks, with the damper open and no fire or
heat. Allow to dry until casings are dry to the touch.

Prepared Beef Summer Sausage

Raise the temperature of the smoker to 120° or 130°F, add smoke chips, and smoke for three to four hours. Raise the temperature to 170°F and cook until the internal temperature reaches 165°F. Shower with cold water. Place sausages back in the cooled-down smoker and hang at room temperature for one to three hours to dry and bloom the sausage.

Peppered Beef Summer Sausage
3 lbs. regular beef (not lean)
2 lbs. pork trimmings
5 tbsps. curing salt
1 ½ tsps. fresh ground black peppercorns
½ tsp. uncrushed peppercorns
½ tsp. ground red pepper
1 tbsp. garlic powder or 5 minced garlic cloves
1 cup cold water

If you like the taste of black pepper, this version will be a favorite. Weigh meats and grind using a $^3/_{16}$ in. plate. Mix spices and pour over ground meat. Blend thoroughly. Place in a covered plastic or glass bowl and refrigerate overnight.

Mix well, roll into logs 1 ½ × 12 ins. long, and wrap in plastic or foil or stuff in 2 ½ in. fibrous casings and refrigerate overnight again. Cook on oven racks at 325°F or smoke at 130°F for two hours. Raise temperature to 160°F and smoke for two more hours. Raise the temperature to 180°F and cook until internal temperature reaches 160°F.

Lamb Summer Sausage

3 lbs. lamb
2 lbs. pork trimmings
5 tbsps. Morton Tender Quick Mix or other cure
1 tbsp black pepper
1 tsp mustard seed
1 tsp marjoram
1 tbsp sugar
1 tbsp garlic powder or 5 minced garlic cloves
1 cup cold water

A mild-flavored summer sausage with the distinct flavor and texture of lamb, this sausage will go well with stronger-flavored cheeses. Weigh and coarse-grind the meats. Mix in the cure. Place in a shallow pan and place in a cooler or refrigerator for three to five days. Remove, add the spices, and re-grind using a ⅛ in. plate. Partial freezing will help with this task. Stuff the sausages into 2 ½ in. fibrous casings.

Place in smoker and smoke at 130°F for two hours. Raise temperature to 160°F and smoke for two to three hours. Raise temperature to 170°F and cook until internal temperature reaches 160° or 170°F.

Easy-Does-It Deer-Season Venison Sausage

3 lbs. venison
2 lbs. pork trimmings
1 tbsp. mustard seed
1 tsp. liquid smoke
5 tbsps. curing salt
1 tsp. black pepper
1 cup cold water

This is a quick and easy sausage to make when you first bring home the venison. Bone off the venison and cut the meat into 1 in. cubes. Refrigerate overnight. Cut the pork into cubes and weigh both meats. Grind both through a $3/16$ in. plate. Mix the cure and spices in a glass bowl and pour over the meat. Mix the meat and spices well, adding the water slowly as you mix. Shape the sausage into rolls and wrap each roll in plastic wrap. Refrigerate overnight. Unwrap the rolls and place on broiler pan. Bake at 325°F until internal temperature reaches 160°F. Store wrapped in the refrigerator for a couple of days, and freeze for longer storage.

Cervelat Summer Sausage

2 lbs. beef chuck

2 lbs. fatty pork butt or pork trimmings

1 lb. beef or pork hearts

1 tsp. ground black pepper

5 tbsps. curing salt

1 ½ tsps. ground coriander

1 tbsp. garlic powder

1 tsp. ground mustard

Cervelat sausage is an extremely popular German sausage that is also popular in Sweden and normally consists of more pork than beef. Larger pieces of pork fat in this recipe make the appearance of this sausage distinctly different from that of other varieties.

Cut the beef chuck and hearts into 1 in. cubes and grind through a ⅛ in. grinder plate. Cut the pork pieces into 1 inch cubes and grind through a ³/₁₆ or ¼ in. plate. Place the meats and seasonings in a tub and mix thoroughly. Stuff the meat into 2 ½ inch synthetic or fibrous casings and place in the refrigerator for forty-eight hours.

Hang the meat on drying racks and dry at room temperature for four to five hours, or place in a smoker on sticks with the damper open until the casings are dry. Raise the temperature of the smoker to 120° to 130°F, add smoke chips, and smoke for three to four hours. Raise the temperature to 170°F and cook until the internal temperature reaches 165°F. Shower with cold water. Place the sausages back in the cooled-down smoker and hang at room temperature for one to three hours to dry and bloom the sausage. This sausage is a good choice for drying after cooking.

Jalapeño-Cheese Venison Summer Sausage

3 lbs. venison

2 lbs. pork trimmings

5 tbsps. cure

1 tbsp. black pepper

1 tsp. mustard seed

1 tsp. marjoram

1 tbsp. sugar

1 tbsp. garlic powder or 5 minced garlic cloves

½ lb. high-temperature jalapeño cheese

If you like a bit of heat with your summer sausage, you'll enjoy both the heat and the tasty addition of cheese. This is a very popular sausage at our deer camps. The cheese must be a high-temperature cheese that will not melt at up to 400°F, so you can smoke and cook the sausage as you would normally. Weigh the meat and cut it into one-inch chunks. Mix the cure and seasonings in a glass or plastic bowl and sprinkle over the meat chunks. Mix the meat and seasonings well. Grind the seasoned meat through a ³/₁₆ in. plate. Place the ground meat in a large bowl or tub and add the cheese, making sure it is well distributed throughout the ground meat. Stuff the meat and cheese into 2 ½ in. fibrous casings.

Hang the sausages on drying racks and dry at room temperature for four to five hours, or place in a smoker on sticks, with the damper open, until the casings are dry. Raise the temperature of the smoker to between 120 and 130°F, add smoke chips, and smoke for three to four hours. Raise the temperature to 170°F and cook until the internal temperature reaches 165°F. Shower with cold water. Place back in the cooled-down smoker and hang at room temperature for one to three hours to dry and bloom the sausage.

Regardless of whether dried, semidried, or hard sausages, they should all be cooked to an internal temperature of at least 160°F.

Want a little variety? Try jalapeño-cheese venison summer sausage.

Special high-temperature cheese is added to the ground meat.

After cooking, sausages should be immediately immersed in ice water to cool them down quickly.

Beef Salami

1 lb beef chuck

1 ½ level teaspoons Morton Tender Quick Mix or Morton
Sugar Cure (Plain) Mix

1 tsp. Morton table salt

(For a spicier version, substitute 1½ tsps Morton Sausage
and Meat Loaf Seasoning Mix.)

½ tsp. mustard seeds

½ tsp. freshly ground black pepper

½ tsp. garlic powder

⅛ tsp. nutmeg

Few drops of liquid smoke, if desired

From the Morton Salt folks, this cooked salami is extremely easy to prepare, and the small amount provides a chance to try your hand at this type of sausage making.

Combine all ingredients, mixing until thoroughly blended. Divide in half. Shape each half into slender rolls about 1 ½ ins. in diameter. Wrap in plastic or foil. Refrigerate overnight.

Unwrap. Bake on a broiler pan at 325°F until a meat thermometer inserted in the center of a roll reads 160°F,

An easy way to make summer sausage is to simply roll the ground and seasoned meat into logs.

Wrap the rolls in plastic wrap and refrigerate overnight to meld flavors and set the sausages.

about fifty to sixty minutes. Store wrapped in refrigerator. Use within three to five days, or freeze for later use.

Smoked Salami
3 lbs. lean chuck beef
2 lbs. fatty pork
3 tbsps. soy protein concentrate
3 tbsps. corn syrup
1 tbsp. ground black pepper
1 ½ tsps. whole black pepper
1 tbsp. garlic powder or 5 minced garlic cloves
5 tbsps. curing salt
1 tbsp. cardamom
1 cup ice water

This is excellent smoked salami that also is cooked in the smoker. The larger pork pieces add to the appearance and flavor. Weigh the meats and keep separate. Grind the pork through a ¼ in. or coarse plate and the beef through a ⅛ in. or fine plate. Mix the meats together and add the other ingredients. Mix well and stuff into 3 ½ ins. fibrous or cellulose casings. Refrigerate the sausages overnight.

Hang the meat on drying racks and dry at room temperature for four to five hours, or place in smoker on sticks with damper open until the casings are dry. Raise the temperature of the smoker to between 120° and 130°F, add smoke chips, and smoke for three to four hours. Raise the temperature to 170°F and cook until the internal temperature reaches 165°F. Shower with cold water. Place back in the cooled down smoker and hang

Unwrap and bake in a 325° oven until the internal temperature of the sausages reaches 160 ° F.

at room temperature for one to three hours to dry and bloom the sausage. This sausage can also be dried after cooking.

Cooked or Smoked Salami

3 lbs. lean beef chuck

2 lbs. pork shoulder butt

½ tsp. Bradley Sugar Cure

1 tsp. black peppercorns, cracked

2 tsps. paprika

1 tsp. ground black pepper

1 tsp. onion powder

1 tsp. garlic powder

½ tsp. nutmeg

½ tsp. allspice

¼ tsp. ground red pepper

¼ cup sherry (optional but recommended)

2 tbsps. light corn syrup

½ cup water

1 cup finely powdered dry skim milk

From the Bradley Smoker folks, this is great smoked salami with lots of flavor. Soak fibrous casings in water for thirty minutes prior to using. Four casings will be required if they are 2 ½ ins. in diameter and about 12 ins. long. Grind the beef and pork through a ³⁄₁₆ in. plate.

Mix the seasonings, cure, water, and powdered milk in a large bowl until the ingredients are perfectly blended. (For a normal salt taste, add the optional 1 tsp. of salt; for a mild taste, omit the salt.) Add the meat to the mixture and mix thoroughly. Knead for about three minutes.

Stuff the sausage mixture into the fibrous casings. Insert the cable probe of an electronic thermometer in the open end of one of the sausages. Close the casing around the probe with butcher's string. Refrigerate the salami overnight.

Remove the sausage from the refrigerator, and place it in a smoker that has been heated to 150°F. Make sure the damper is fully open while drying the surface of the casings. Maintain this temperature with no smoke until the casing is dry to the touch. (Alternatively, dry the casings in front of an electric fan.) Raise the smoker temperature

Some "hard" sausages, such as salami and pepperoni, are traditionally dried under the right conditions. The Sausage Maker, Inc., has a complete kit for creating these traditional sausages.

Although many hard sausages are stuffed into casings and smoked or dried, there are also easier ways to make these kinds of sausages (including pepperoni).

to 160°F, add the Bradley wood bisquettes, and smoke for three to six hours. If you wish to cook the sausage in the smoker, raise the temperature to 180°F and cook until the internal temperature is 160°F.

Instead of final cooking in the smoker, the sausages may be cooked by steaming. After smoking the sausages for three to six hours, wrap each sausage in plastic food wrap (optional), and steam until the internal temperature is 160°F. A steamer may be improvised by using a large pan with an elevated rack inside, covered with a lid.

As soon as the cooking is finished, chill the sausage in cold water until the internal temperature drops below 100°F. Refrigerate overnight before using.

Morton Salt Pepperoni

1 lb. lean ground beef (chuck)

1 ½ level teaspoons Morton Tender Quick Mix or Morton
Sugar Cure (Plain) Mix

1 tsp. liquid smoke

¾ tsp. freshly ground black pepper

½ tsp. mustard seed

½ tsp. fennel seed, slightly crushed

¼ tsp. crushed red pepper

¼ tsp. anise seed

¼ tsp. garlic powder

Homemade pizzas taste even better with pepperoni sausage you've made yourself. The small batch in this recipe, from Morton Salt, also provides a quick and easy way of creating a semidry "hard sausage."

Grind beef through a ³/₁₆ in. plate. Combine all ingredients, mixing until thoroughly blended. Divide mixture in half. Shape each half into a slender roll about 1 ½ ins. in diameter. Wrap in plastic or foil. Refrigerate overnight. Unwrap rolls and place on a broiler pan. Bake at 325°F until a meat thermometer inserted in the center of the roll reads 160°F, about fifty to sixty minutes. Store wrapped in the refrigerator. Use within three to five days, or freeze for later use.

Bradley Smoker Wild Game Pastrami Sausage

4 lbs. wild game meat (venison, elk, moose)

1 lb. pork fat

½ tsp. Bradley Sugar Cure (do not use more than this amount)

1 tsp. salt (optional)

4 tsps. light corn syrup

4 tsps. black peppercorns, cracked

1 tsp. onion powder

1 tsp. garlic powder

½ tsp. cayenne

½ tsp. paprika

½ tsp. oregano

¼ tsp. allspice

¼ tsp. ginger powder

½ cup water

1 cup fine powdered skim milk

Using a combination of smoking with the Bradley Smoker and cooking in an oven, this is an easy and spicy pastrami recipe. Soak 2 ½ in. fibrous casings for thirty minutes before stuffing. Grind the meats through a ³⁄₁₆ in. plate.

Mix the seasonings, cure, water, and powdered milk in a large bowl until the ingredients are perfectly blended. (For a normal salt taste, add the optional 1 tsp. of salt; for a mild salt taste, omit the salt.) Add the meat to the mixture and mix thoroughly. Knead for about three minutes.

Many hard sausages are also smoked for flavor or hot-smoked for cooking.

Stuff the sausage mixture into the fibrous casings. Insert the cable probe of an electronic thermometer in the open end of one of the sausages. Close the casing around the probe with butcher's string. Refrigerate the salami overnight.

Remove the sausage from the refrigerator and place it in a smoker heated to 150°F. Make sure the damper is fully open while drying the surface of the casings. Maintain this temperature with no smoke until the casing is dry to the touch. (Alternatively, dry the casings in front of an electric fan.)

Raise the smoker temperature to 160°F, add the Bradley wood bisquettes, and smoke for three to six hours. If you wish to cook the sausage in the smoker, raise the temperature to 180°F and cook until the internal temperature is 160°F.

Instead of final cooking in the smoker, the sausages may be cooked by steaming. After smoking for three to six hours, wrap each sausage in plastic food wrap (optional), and secure the ends with a wire bread-bag tie. Steam the sausages until the internal temperature is 160°F. A steamer may be improvised by using a large pan with an elevated rack inside, covered with a lid.

As soon as the cooking is finished, chill the sausage in cold water until the internal temperature drops below 100°F. Refrigerate overnight before using.

Dried Sausage Sticks (Slim Jims)

1 lb. venison

1 tbsp. Morton Tender Quick Mix

¼ tsp. black pepper

½ tsp. onion powder

¼ tsp. garlic powder

¼ tsp. Worcestershire sauce

1 tsp. crushed red pepper

1 tsp. liquid smoke

Premixed seasonings, such as a pepperoni mix, make it easy to make your own Slim Jims.

Use a jerky gun or, in this case, an extruder on the LEM grinder to easily extrude the sausage sticks.

My nephew Morgan created this great jerky-style sausage recipe that can be made in small batches. Simply take a pound of previously ground venison or other red meat (burger) out of the freezer, thaw, and mix in the ingredients. Cover with a plastic wrap in a plastic or glass bowl and refrigerate overnight. The liquid smoke isn't added to the ground meat; instead, it's sprayed on during the drying process.

To make the Slim Jims, extrude the ground and seasoned meat through a jerky gun (using the small round nozzle) onto oiled cookie sheets, or a jerky screen for oven drying, or dehydrator trays for drying. Morgan dries the batch long enough to set the top side, then sprays that side with liquid smoke.

Halfway through the drying process, he turns the strips over on the dehydrator trays and sprays the other side. Morgan says the liquid smoke isn't lost in the ground-meat mixture, and the sausage has a fresher, smoked flavor. You can also brush on liquid smoke with a pastry brush. The meat must be dried/cooked to an internal temperature of 160°F.

CHAPTER 8

Cooked Sausages

Although many sausages are cooked or smoke-cooked, fresh sausage must still be cooked before consuming. Other sausages are designated "cooked," meaning they are already cooked and ready to eat. These sausages include the popular frankfurters or hot dogs, as well as numerous luncheon meats. Some, such as hot dogs, are usually heated and served hot, while luncheon meats are served cold. The cooked, ready-to-eat sausages usually require more effort to produce. Most are made of very finely ground meats, which require grinding through a fine plate at least two—and, preferably, three or more—times. Or the meats can be emulsified using a food processor. All of these traditional sausages must be kept refrigerated or frozen.

Traditional American Hot Dogs

3 lbs. lean beef

2 lbs. pork butt or pork trimmings

5 tbsps. Morton Tender Quick Mix

½ tsp. ground white pepper

½ tsp. garlic powder

½ tsp. ground celery seed

1 ½ tsps. mace

½ tsp. coriander

½ tsp. onion powder

1 tbsp. ground mustard

3 tbsps. soy protein concentrate

1 tbsp. paprika

4 tbsps. corn syrup

Making your own cooked sausages, such as hot dogs and luncheon meats, is also a lot of fun and allows you to control the source of your ingredients.

Many cooked sausages must be finely ground. This can be done with several grindings or by using a quality food processor. Adding a bit of water during processing helps.

Almost any combination of meats can be used for hot dogs. Packing-plant hot dogs are made from all the trimmings you can imagine, and then some. You should, however, stick to the proper proportions of lean and fat. If using wild game meat, make sure you cut off all fat. Again, this can be a clean-out-your-freezer-of-meats situation, but remember that the quality of the hot dogs will only be as good as the quality of meats used. Freezer-burned or dehydrated meat will not make good hot dogs.

Hot dogs are one of the more difficult sausages to make. This is primarily because of the number of times the meats need grinding and the fact that you need to stuff the finely ground and cured meat into small casings. You will need a good-quality stuffer with the correct-size stuffing tubes.

Grind all the meats through a fine, ⅛ in. plate. Partially freeze, cut into 1 in. chunks, and re-grind. For even finer meats, repeat the process or, for the last step, emulsify the meats using a food processor. In this case you will probably need to add up to a cup of water to the ground meat for easier processing. Make sure the meat is kept well chilled and not allowed to become warm during the grinding and processing. Refrigerate or chill between each step.

Mix all ingredients with the processed meat and knead or mix for two to three minutes. Stuff into small pork casings or sheep casings or, for larger hot dogs, large pork casings. (Alternatively, you can stuff the meat into 24-mm collagen hot dog casings.)

If you desire smoked hot dogs, place them in a smoker, making sure they do not touch each other, and allow the casings to air-dry. Dry for about an hour at room temperature for natural casings or about a half hour for collagen casings. Or hang the raw links in a 150°F smoker until the outside is dry to the touch, which will require at least thirty minutes. Make sure the damper is fully open. Raise the temperature gradually to 180°F. If you choose to add smoke flavor, add the smoke chips at this time. Close the damper most of the way to reduce the airflow, thereby reducing dehydration. Hot-smoke at this temperature until the internal temperature is 160°F.

Remove the links from the smoker and shower them with cold water until the internal temperature is below 110°F. Hang at room temperature for about thirty minutes. Refrigerate overnight to allow the smoke flavor to mellow before eating. Freeze the links that will not be consumed within two days.

Steam-cooking or simmering will result in less shrinkage than cooking in the smoker. If you want a smoked flavor, smoke at 130°F only until the hot dogs turn a golden brown. Hot dogs do not have to be smoked for flavor. Immediately remove the hot dogs and steam or simmer until the internal temperature is 160°F. Immediately shower with cold water until the internal temperature reaches 100° to 110°F. Hang at room temperature for about thirty minutes, and then refrigerate.

Or, after smoking, poach the franks in 180°F water until the internal temperature is 160°F. Shower with cold water and refrigerate uncovered. Hot dogs do not have to be smoked for flavor, merely steam-cooked.

After the sausage is chilled, package them in plastic bags. Freeze the links that will not be consumed within two days.

Skinless Wieners

You can also make skinless hot dogs by using LEM nonedible hot dog casings. Grind meat into a fine emulsion and add seasonings and ingredients. Then use one of the following preparation methods:

1. Stuff casings and place in 180°F water and cook for thirty minutes or until the internal temperature of meat reaches 165°F.

2. Place filled casings in smoker with a pan of water in smoker to add humidity and cook at 180°F until the internal temperature of meat reaches 165°F. (Do not cook in oven.)

When cooking is completed, immediately plunge hot dogs in ice water for two to three minutes to prevent shriveling. Refrigerate or freeze in casings.

Before eating, peel off the casings. Boil, grill, or broil the finished hot dogs. One strand makes approximately twenty-eight hot dogs, ⅞ in. in diameter.

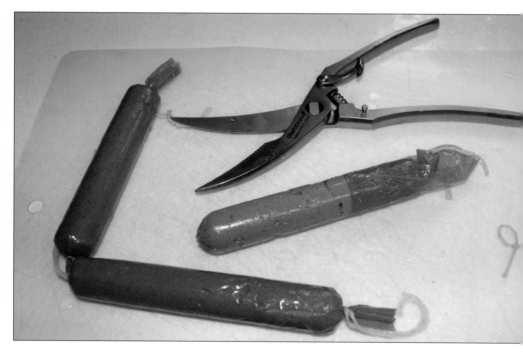

You can also make skinless hot dogs using nonedible hot dog casings. Stuff the casings, cook, and then peel off the casings before consuming.

When a recipe calls for added water, mix the spices with the water and then pour over and mix with the meat.

All-Beef Hot Dogs

5 lbs. beef chuck

1 to 3 tbsps. salt

1 tsp. garlic powder

1 tsp. onion powder

1 tbsp. coriander

2 tbsps. sugar

1 ½ tsps. mace

½ tsp. ground red pepper

1 tsp. liquid smoke

1 tsp. finely ground black pepper

3 tbsps soy protein concentrate

1 cup cold water

1 tbsp. paprika

This recipe makes a very lean hot dog with lots of flavor. Grind meat three times through a fine plate. Chill or refrigerate. Mix the soy protein concentrate in the water and stir in the spices. Pour over the ground meat and mix well for about three minutes, making sure the seasonings are well distributed. Stuff into sheep or hog casings or 24-mm collagen casings, depending on whether you want small or large hot dogs. Place in a smoker and smoke at 130°F only until you get a rich, orange color.

Cook in water heated to 180°F until the hot dogs float and the internal temperature is 160°F. Immediately cool in ice water. Hang to dry for about thirty minutes, then place in a refrigerator overnight. Consume immediately or place in plastic bags and freeze.

Bradley Smoker Old-Fashioned Frankfurters

2 lbs. beef chuck

3 lbs. fatty pork butt

14 ft. small-diameter hog casings

½ tsp. Bradley Sugar Cure

1 tbsp. ground coriander

2 tsps. onion powder

2 tsps. black pepper, finely ground

1 tsp. salt (optional)

1 tsp. ground mustard

½ tsp. garlic powder

½ tsp. marjoram

½ tsp. mace

2 eggs, well beaten
²⁄₃ cup water
1 cup finely powdered skim milk

From the Bradley Smoker folks, this is a great way of making your own tasty frankfurters. Grind the meat through a ⅛ in. or fine plate. If the meat is ground twice, it will be finer the second time. Chill the meat thoroughly.

Mix the Bradley Sugar Cure, seasonings, water, and powdered skim milk in an 8 qt. stainless-steel mixing bowl until they are thoroughly blended and the powdered milk has dissolved. (For a normal taste, add the optional 1 tsp. of salt; for a mild taste, omit the salt.)

Add the meat and mix well with hands (about three minutes). Chill again. Stuff the sausage in hog casings and twist the sausage rope into links. Refrigerate at least one hour (overnight is better). Continue processing by using one of the two options described below. (Frankfurters are traditionally smoked.)

Option 1: If you wish to hot-smoke the frankfurters, hang the raw links in a 150°F smoker until the outside is dry to the touch (this will require at least thirty minutes). Make sure the damper is fully open. Raise the temperature gradually to 180°F. Close the damper most of the way to reduce the airflow, thereby reducing dehydration. Hot-smoke at this temperature until the internal temperature is 160°F. Remove the links from the smoker and spray them with cold water until the internal temperature is below 110°F. Hang at room temperature for about thirty minutes. Refrigerate overnight before eating; this allows the smoke flavor to mellow. Freeze the links that will not be consumed within two days.

Option 2: Steam-cooking will result in less shrinkage than cooking in the smoker. Follow the directions above for hot-smoking, but remove the links from the smoker when the internal temperature is about 135°F. Steam the sausage until the internal temperature is 160°F. Spray with cold water, then hang at room temperature for about thirty minutes, and refrigerate.

Or, after smoking, poach the franks in 180°F water until the internal temperature is 160°F. Eat immediately, or spray with water and refrigerate uncovered. After the sausages are chilled, package them in plastic bags. Freeze the links that will not be consumed within two days.

Ring or Large Bologna

3 lbs. lean beef or venison
2 lbs. pork butt
5 tbsps. Morton Tender Quick Mix
2 tsps. finely ground white pepper
1 tbsp. paprika
½ tsp. nutmeg
1 tsp. allspice
1 tsp. onion powder
1 tsp. garlic powder
3 tbsps. soy protein concentrate

If you want to create a traditional large-size or ring-size bologna, this recipe is a good choice. Once you've tried it and "tweaked" it to suit your taste buds, you may want to double the recipe for a larger supply of summer luncheon meat. The type of bologna depends on the type of casing used. The large, synthetic casing shown from The Sausage Maker, Inc., makes this traditional large bologna.

Weigh and grind the meats through a ⅛ in. plate. Mix the meats together and chill in a refrigerator, or partially freeze and re-grind. For a finer, emulsified bologna, repeat this step, or run through a food processor.

Mix the meat and other ingredients thoroughly. Stuff into traditional beef rounds or 2 ½ in. protein-lined collagen casings for ring bologna. For large-style bologna, use beef bungs, 4 ⅞ in. red bologna synthetic

Hot dogs and luncheon meats are traditionally cooked by steaming or poaching but may also be smoked for flavor.

or muslin casings. Make sure the sausage is stuffed tightly into the casings and prick any air pockets with a sharp needle. Rinse any fat or meat particles from outside the casings. If possible, allow stuffed casings to hang in a cool place overnight (40° to 45°F), or place in a refrigerator or cooler.

Place on smoker racks or sticks and allow the stuffed casings to dry for about an hour in the smoker or in front of an electric fan. Or place in a smoker preheated to 130 or 135°F, with the dampers wide open, and dry for about a half hour. If you want a smoked flavor, add wood chips and continue cold-smoking at 130° to 135°F for two to three hours, or until the sausage has a rich brown color. To hot-smoke, increase temperature to 180°F and cook until the internal temperature reaches 160°F. Remove from the smoker and spray with cold water until the internal temperature drops to 100° or 110°F.

For cooked bologna, place the smoked sausage immediately into water heated to 180°F and simmer until the sausages float or squeak when the pressure of the thumb and forefinger on the casings is suddenly released. Make sure the internal temperature of all the sausages reaches 160°F. Plunge the cooked sausages into cold water to chill. Place in a refrigerator or cooler until the internal temperature reaches below 50°F, and then refrigerate or freeze.

Bradley Smoker German Bologna

3 lbs. lean beef or game meat

1 lb. lean pork

1 lb. pork fat

½ tsp. Bradley Sugar Cure (do not use more than this amount)

2 tsps. black pepper, finely ground

1 tsp. salt (optional)

1 tsp. ground mustard seed

1 tsp. ground celery seed

1 tsp. garlic powder

½ tsp. coriander

½ tsp. nutmeg

½ cup chilled water

1 cup finely powdered skim milk

It's fun to create your own bologna sandwich meat, and you can use a variety of meats, including beef, venison, elk, or moose. Game meat should be trimmed of all fat before grinding. Grind all meat through a fine plate. Pass all meat through the grinder twice for a finer bologna. Chill the meat thoroughly.

Mix the Bradley Sugar Cure, seasonings, water, and powdered milk in a large bowl until the ingredients are uniform. (For a normal salt taste, add the optional 1 tsp. of salt; for a mild taste, omit the salt.) Add the meat to the seasoning mixture and blend well by kneading for about three minutes.

Stuff the sausage into fibrous casings. Insert the cable probe of an electronic thermometer in the open end of one of the sausages, and close the casing around the probe with butcher's string. Refrigerate the stuffed sausages overnight.

Remove the sausage from the refrigerator and place it in a smoker that has been heated to 150°F. Maintain this temperature with no smoke until the casing is dry to the touch. (Alternatively, dry the casing in front of an electric fan.) Raise the temperature to 160°F and smoke for three to six hours. If you wish to cook the sausage in the smoker, raise the temperature to 180°F and smoke until the internal temperature is 160°F.

After smoking the sausages for three to six hours (but not cooking in the smoker), wrap them in plastic food wrap (optional) and steam them until the internal temperature is 160°F. A steamer may be improvised by using a large pan with an elevated rack inside, covered with a lid. As soon as the cooking is finished, chill the sausages overnight before using.

Country-Style Bologna

6 lbs. boneless pork trimmings

4 lbs. boneless beef trimmings

2 cups ice water

½ cup Morton Tender Quick Mix or Morton Sugar Cure (Plain) Mix

2 tbsps. sugar

1 tbsp. ground white pepper

1 tbsp. ground coriander

1 tbsp. ground mace

1 tsp. onion powder

2 cups nonfat dry milk powder

2 tbsps. liquid smoke (optional)

3- to 4-in. (in diameter) cellulose or fibrous casings

Another excellent and tasty Morton Salt recipe, this is a very easy and proven bologna for first-time sausage makers. Cut meat into 1 in. cubes. Grind through a ¼ in. plate. In large bowl, mix ground meat with remaining ingredients; cover and refrigerate overnight.

Re-grind meat mixture through ⅛ in. plate. Stuff into casings and tie ends. Prick air pockets with a clean needle.

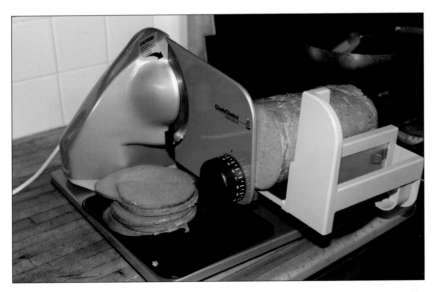

Bologna and luncheon meats (i.e., pickle loaf) are great recipes for home sausage makers to try. Use a Chef'sChoice meat slicer to slice the cooled bologna.

Place bologna in a large pot and add water to cover. Bring to a boil and reduce heat. Simmer until fully cooked or until internal temperature of 160°F is obtained. Cool bologna in ice water for twelve to fifteen minutes. Store in refrigerator or freeze.

Pickle Loaf

3 lbs. lean beef

2 lbs. pork butt

5 tbsps. Morton Tender Quick Mix

1 tbspn. powdered dextrose

½ tsp. ground ginger

½ tsp. onion powder

¼ tsp. mace

1 tsp. finely ground white pepper

6 oz sweet pickles, chopped

6 oz pimento peppers, chopped

1 cup nonfat dry milk

1 cup ice water

Another very popular luncheon meat "sausage" is pickle loaf. This is basically a bologna with the addition of chopped sweet pickles and pimento peppers. You can make up your own pickle loaf and add different ingredients to suit your taste.

Weigh and grind the meats through a ⅛ in. plate. Mix the meats together and chill in the refrigerator, or partially freeze, and re-grind. For a finer, emulsified bologna, repeat this step or run through a food processor.

Mix the meat and ingredients thoroughly and stuff into 6 in. synthetic or muslin casings. Make sure the sausage is stuffed tightly into the casings and prick any air pockets with a sharp needle. Rinse off any fat or meat particles from the outside of the casings. If possible, allow them to hang in a cool place overnight, 40° to 45°F, or place in a refrigerator or cooler.

Fill a large pot with warm water. You should have enough water to cover the sausages, with about 3 ins. to spare. Carefully lower the sausages into the water and weigh them down with a heavy plate to keep them submerged. When the water begins to simmer, maintain the heat at 180°F and simmer the sausages until the internal temperature reaches 160°F. A remote temperature probe makes this task much easier. (Incidentally, a gas fish cooker makes this easy to do outdoors.)

Remove the sausages and immediately place them in a tub filled with water and ice. As the ice melts, add more. The idea is to chill the bologna as quickly as possible down to 100°F. Dip the cased sausages in hot water to remove all surface grease, then hang them on a rack to dry. If you wish a smoked flavor, cold-smoke them at 120°F for about two to three hours before cooking.

Venison Baked Bologna

2 lbs. venison
2 tbsps. Morton Tender Quick Mix
$\frac{1}{8}$ tsp. garlic powder
$\frac{1}{4}$ tsp. onion powder

1 tsp. liquid smoke
½ tsp. black pepper, finely ground
¼ cup water

This recipe comes from my friend George Williams, a serious deer hunter. If you like the taste of pure venison, this is a great choice. If you already have some ground venison, this is a good "experiment" sausage. You can, however, add 1 lb. of lean pork for a smoother bologna. Grind through a ¼ in. plate, mix ingredients, then grind through a ⅛ in. plate. Divide and shape into two rolls and wrap in plastic wrap. Refrigerate for twenty-four hours, remove plastic wrap, and bake in a 325°F oven for forty-five minutes or until an internal temperature of 160°F is reached.

Braunschweiger

2 ½ lbs. pork liver
2 ½ lbs. fatty pork trimmings
5 tbsps. Morton Tender Quick Mix
4 tbsps. corn syrup
½ tsp. ground ginger
½ tsp. ground nutmeg
¼ tsp. ground cloves
¼ tsp. ground allspice
¼ tsp. ground sage
¼ tsp. ground marjoram
1 tbsp. onion powder
1 tsp. finely ground white pepper
3 tablespoons soy protein concentrate

If you like the taste of liver luncheon meats, try your hand at liverwurst or braunschweiger.

Braunschweiger is typically stuffed in synthetic or collagen "ring-style" casings.

If you want to try your hand at making a classic German sausage, and you like the taste of liver sausage, this is a good choice. The original meat was usually pork snouts or heads, fatty pork. You can substitute half pork trimmings and half pork fat. Grind meats through a fine or ⅛ in. plate. Partially freeze the meat, cut into 1 in. cubes, grind, and repeat, or emulsify in a food processor.

Chill the meat, then add the spices and mix thoroughly. Stuff the meats into 2 ¾ in. collagen or synthetic casings, or you can use a sewn muslin casing.

Fill a large pot with warm water. You should have enough water to cover the sausages, with about 3 ins. to spare. Carefully lower the sausages into the water and weight them down with a heavy plate to keep them submerged. When the water begins to simmer, maintain the heat at 180°F and simmer the sausages until the internal temperature reaches 160°F. A remote temperature probe makes this task much easier.

Remove the sausages and immediately place in a tub filled with water and ice. As the ice melts, add more. The idea is to chill the braunschweiger as quickly as possible down to 100°F. Dip the cased sausages in hot water and remove all surface grease. Then hang on a rack to dry. If you wish a smoked flavor, cold-smoke at 120°F for about two to three hours before cooking.

Liverwurst
2 ½ lbs. pork liver
1 ½ lbs. pork butt

½ lb. pork fat
1 tsp. onion powder
½ tsp. ground mace
1 tsp. dried marjoram
½ tsp. ground allspice
½ tsp. ground coriander
2 tsps. sugar
1 tsp. ground white pepper
4 tbsps. coarse or canning salt
1 tsp. paprika
1 cup nonfat dry milk powder
1 cup ice water

Another very popular German sausage, this is also a great recipe for utilizing hog's liver from butchering days. This is a very finely ground, creamy-style sausage, and it takes a lot of grinding and/or processing, but if you like liver luncheon meat, it's worth it.

Remove veins and stringy tissue from liver. Cut liver, fat, and meat into 1 in. chunks. Chill and grind through a fine plate. Partially freeze and re-grind. Add the spices to the water and mix thoroughly. Partially freeze and re-grind, then partially freeze and re-grind again, or emulsify in a food processor.

Stuff the liverwurst into 4 in. synthetic or collagen casings or into sewn muslin casings. Make sure the meat is packed tightly into the casings.

Fill a large pot with warm water. You should have enough water to cover the sausages, with about 3 in. to

THE COMPLETE GUIDE TO SAUSAGE MAKING

spare. Carefully lower the sausages into the water and weight them down with a heavy plate to keep them submerged. When the water begins to simmer, maintain the heat at 180°F and simmer the sausages until the internal temperature reaches 160°F. A remote temperature probe makes this task much easier. (Incidentally, a gas fish cooker makes this easy to do outdoors.)

Remove the sausages and immediately place in a tub filled with water and ice. As the ice melts, add more. The idea is to chill the liverwurst as quickly as possible down to between 100° and 110°F. Dip the cased sausages in hot water and remove all surface grease. Then hang them on a rack to dry. If you wish a smoked flavor, cold-smoke them at 120°F for two to three hours before cooking.

CHAPTER 9

Specialty Sausages

Specialty sausages include low-fat or "diet" sausages as well as a variety of cooked-meat varieties. Specialty sausages also include a number of "loaf" dishes, such as head cheese, liver loaf, scrapple, and others. Most of these are dishes prepared in the kitchen rather than produced as sausage. One specialty sausage I distinctly remember is head cheese, which was a hog-butchering specialty of our family—one I don't remember with fondness. First, the hog heads had to be cleaned and prepared for cooking. Mom would then cook the heads all day on an old coal-oil stove down in the basement. This very distinct cooking smell permeated the entire house.

A number of specialty sausages can also be made. For the home sausage maker, this includes head cheese (or souse), scrapple (or goetta), and liver loaf.

Head Cheese or Souse

3 lbs. meat (mostly from the head and neck bones, but you can also utilize other trimmings, such as feet, tongue, tail, and so forth)

1 large onion, chopped

Salt and ground pepper to taste

Other spices such as garlic and ground red pepper, to taste

Like many other specialty sausages, head cheese is a way of utilizing the less-desired trimmings and parts of a hog. Because it takes a bit of time and effort, head cheese was usually made a day or two after the butchering, the meat kept refrigerated or cooled at 42° to 45°F until it was time to make the sausage. Our family always butchers in January, so we have several days of cold weather to "work up" the meat.

The first step is to split the head in half and remove the eyes and ears. Clean out the nasal passages and chop off the teeth. If you don't, they will fall out when the meat is cooked. Place the head and other bony pieces in a large pot or kettle and simmer until the meat falls off the bones. You might consider doing this outside, using a fish or turkey fryer for the heat source. Remove the bones, allowing them to cool enough to handle and pick off the meat. Strain the liquid through a kitchen strainer. Remove any bones and small meat pieces. Set the liquid aside.

Sprinkle salt and pepper over the meat, add the onion, and grind all through a fine plate. Add some of the strained liquid back to moisten the meat; place in a pan and bring to a boil. Simmer for fifteen to twenty minutes, until mixture thickens. Pour the cooked mixture into a pan and cover with plastic wrap. Refrigerate.

When cool, slice into sandwich slices like lunch meat. Our favorite method of eating is on a wheat-bread sandwich with butter lathered on the bread.

Scrapple or Goetta

3 lbs. meat (mostly from the head and neck bones, but you can also utilize other trimmings, such as feet, tongue, tail, and so forth)
1 cup cereal (cornmeal or oatmeal)
Salt and black pepper to taste
½ tsp. sweet marjoram
¼ tsp. sage
½ tsp. onion powder
A pinch of mace, nutmeg, and red pepper (if desired)

Scrapple is basically a head-cheese style of sausage, using head meat and other trimmings, with a cereal added (either cornmeal or oatmeal). If oatmeal is used the dish is called goetta. Often a bit of flour is also added.

Prepare the meat in the same manner as for head cheese, cooking it and picking the meat from the bones, then grinding it. Reserve 4 cups of liquid. If you don't have enough liquid, add water or a light stock if necessary. Add cereal to a bit of the cooled liquid and mix so no lumps are formed. Pour the liquid into a pot and add the premixed cereal/liquid and ground meat. Stir together and boil for about thirty minutes, stirring frequently to prevent sticking. Add in the seasonings at the end of the cooking time. Pour into a bread pan and place the scrapple in the refrigerator to cool. Once cool and firm, cut into slices. Scrapple is usually served as a breakfast dish. Sauté in butter and serve hot with maple syrup.

German Grits

1 beef heart
1 beef tongue
5 lbs. neck bones or short ribs
1 large onion, chopped
2 cloves garlic, chopped
Salt and black pepper to taste
¼ tsp. mustard seed
2 cups pearled barley
1 cup old-fashioned rolled oats

This breakfast dish utilizes the trimmings from butchering a beef. Cook heart and tongue in one pot. Cook the neck or rib bones in another. Add enough water in each pot to cover the meat and simmer until the meat easily comes off the bones and the heart and tongue are thoroughly cooked (about two to three hours). Remove meat from broth, allow both to cool, and pick meat off the bones. Skim off any fat that comes to the surface of the broth. Grind all the meat through a fine ⅛ in. plate. Strain the broth and remove any bone pieces. Add the spices to the broth and simmer for one hour. Add the pearled barley and simmer until it becomes plump. Mix in the cooked ground meats. Add enough old-fashioned rolled oats to soak up excess broth. Season to taste with salt and pepper. Form grits into patties and fry. If you want a beefier taste, add beef bouillon cubes to the broth.

Liver Sausage

8 lbs. pork trimmings

2 lbs. pork or calf liver

½ cup plus 2 tablespoons Morton Tender Quick Mix

2 tsps. ground black pepper

Sage, allspice, and ground red pepper (½ to 1 tsp. each or to taste)

This traditional Morton Salt recipe has been around for a long time. Old-timers like my grandparents used this recipe to utilize just about everything from the pig but the squeal. Head meat, tongues, hearts, and all kinds of trimmings are used.

Slow-cook or simmer the bones until the meat can be easily removed. Strain to remove meat from broth and save the broth. Remove all blood vessels from the liver and score deeply. Place the liver pieces in boiling water for ten to fifteen minutes. Chill meat and liver pieces. Grind through a fine plate twice. Mix the meats and spices. Add enough of the saved liquid to the mixture to create a soft (but not wet) texture.

Many of these sausages require grinding . . .

. . . and then partial freezing, cutting the meat into chunks and re-grinding.

Stuff the sausage into muslin or synthetic casings. Cover the sausages with warm water and simmer at 180°F until the sausage floats and/or the internal temperature reaches 160°F. Plunge the cooked sausages into cold water to chill immediately. Hang them in a cool place to drain. Use the sausage immediately or freeze for later use.

English-Style Liver Loaf

1 ½ lbs. pork liver
½ lb. pork fat
1 tsp. garlic powder
2 tsps. dehydrated, chopped onion
1 tsp. chopped parsley
1 tsp. dried sage
1 tsp. black pepper
2 tsps. salt
¼ tsp. nutmeg
¼ tsp. cloves
¼ tsp. ground ginger
1 cup dry whole-wheat bread crumbs
Cooking spray

This is an old-fashioned liver loaf that's great sliced and served on bread. Cut out all the veins and tough membranes from the liver. Grind the liver and pork fat through a fine (⅛ in.) plate. Partially freeze and grind again through a fine plate. Stir in the spices and bread crumbs and mix well. The mixture should be slightly runny but should still stand up when dropped from a spoon. Add more bread crumbs if necessary.

Many specialty sausages, such as liver loaf, are simply made into loaves and baked in the oven.

Spray an ovenproof glass or casserole dish with cooking spray. Pack the mixture into the dish, making sure it is packed down tightly, and then cover tightly. If you wish additional flavor, lay a few strips of thinly sliced bacon over the top. Set the casserole in a pan of water and bake in a 350° oven until the juices run clear (about an hour).

Remove from the oven, cover with plastic wrap, and refrigerate overnight. Unmold from the dish and cut into thin slices. Must be consumed immediately or frozen. If freezing, do not slice until ready to use.

Light Italian Sausage

2 lbs. boneless pork shoulder or pork trimmings

1 lb. boneless chicken

2 tbsps. well-seasoned chicken broth

1 tbsp. coarse or canning salt (or to taste)

1 large garlic clove, minced

1 tsp crushed oregano

2 tsps. chopped basil

1 tsp. marjoram

1 cup dried whole-wheat bread crumbs

A light and mild Italian sausage for white-meat lovers, this low-fat, fresh sausage goes great in a wide variety of dishes, and it's quick and easy to make. Cut the pork into 1 in. cubes. Skin and debone legs and thighs of four whole chickens (or enough to make up 1 lb. of boneless chicken) and cut into 1 in. cubes. Grind pork and chicken together through a fine plate. Add the garlic clove and grind a second time through a fine plate. Add the broth, spices, and bread crumbs and mix well together with moistened hands.

Form into patties, cover with waxed paper, and refrigerate overnight, or stuff into casings and refrigerate overnight. To use, fry or bake as a stuffing. This is a fresh sausage, so use immediately or freeze for later use.

Turkey Hot Dogs

5 lbs. raw, boned-out turkey or chicken meat (with some fat)

1 ½ to 2 cups of turkey or chicken stock

5 tbsps. Morton Tender Quick Mix

1 ½ tsps. finely ground white pepper

1 ½ cups all-purpose flour (or coarse-ground durum wheat)

1 cup nonfat dry milk powder or 3 tablespoons soy protein concentrate

2 tbsp. powdered dextrose

1 cup ice water

If you prefer not to eat red meat, you can still make up your own delicious hot dogs using turkey, chicken, or both. (A hot dog made of all turkey meat is more solid than one made of chicken.)

Debone the turkey or chicken and cut into 1 in. cubes. Chill or partially freeze all meat to 30° or 32°F. Grind

You can make sausages such as hot dogs from poultry or add poultry to make "lite" sausages.

through a fine plate and then chill again and re-grind. Thoroughly mix in the flour and dry milk and then add the seasonings to the liquid mix. Mix the liquid with the meat. Place a little of the meat in a food processor and process to emulsify. Gradually add a little of the stock as you process. When all meat has been processed, chill for an hour or so, and then stuff into sheep or small hog casings. This is also a great recipe for skinless dogs using the LEM plastic casings.

Place in a smoker and smoke at 130°F only until you achieve a rich, orange color. Remove from the smoker. Cover the hot dogs with warm water and heat to 180°F until they float and the internal temperature is 165°F. Immediately chill in ice water. Hang them to dry for about thirty minutes, and then place in a refrigerator overnight. Consume immediately or place in plastic bags and freeze.

Wild Goose Salami
3 lbs. wild goose breast meat
2 lbs. pork butt
1 tsp. garlic powder
1 tsp. onion powder
2 tsps. finely ground black pepper
5 tbsps. Morton Tender Quick Mix
1 tsp. ground mustard seed
1 tsp. ground celery seed
2 or more teaspoons liquid smoke

Wild geese, particularly snow geese, have become an increasingly common wildlife problem and even a hazard in many areas. As a result, the hunting season and bag limits are generous. Wild goose meat, however, is dark, often tough, and hard to cook. Making the meat into salami is an excellent way of utilizing this valuable wild meat.

Grind meat through a fine, $\frac{1}{8}$ in. plate. Mix all spices (except the liquid smoke flavoring) into the meat. Divide the meat into fourths, shape into logs, brush the exterior of the logs in liquid smoke, and wrap in plastic wrap. Refrigerate overnight. Place on a wire rack and cook in a 325° oven or smoke/cook in a smoker until the internal temperature reaches 165°F. The sausage can also be stuffed into 2 ½ in. synthetic casings. If stuffing the meat into casings, mix the liquid smoke into the sausage. If smoke/cooking the sausage, leave out the liquid smoke. Refrigerate or freeze until consumed.

Potato Sausage

3 lbs. beef
2 lbs. pork
1 tsp. coarse-ground pepper
1 qt. grated (raw) potatoes
3 large onions (ground)
½ tsp. ground allspice
2 tbsps. Morton Tender Quick Mix

A number of recipes are available for this popular dish, some using only pork, others pork and beef. This recipe uses a combination, but pork and venison will also work. Grind the meats and onions through a fine, $\frac{1}{8}$ in. plate.

Place the ground meats, potatoes, and spices in a large bowl or pan and mix thoroughly by hand. Stuff the mixture into synthetic or muslin casings. Cover the sausages with warm, salted water and simmer on the stovetop until the internal temperature reaches 160°F. This sausage must be refrigerated and consumed immediately or frozen for later use.

To serve, slice into half-inch-thick slices and fry or place on a cookie sheet and brown in the oven at 375°F for about ten minutes.